New Orleans

BY THE BOWL

New Orleans

BY THE BOWL

Gumbos, Jambalayas, Soups, and Stews

John DeMers with Andrew Jaeger

TEN SPEED PRESS

Berkeley | Toronto

Copyright © 2003 by John DeMers
All rights reserved. No part of this book may be reproduced
in any form, except brief excerpts for the purpose of review,
without written permission of the publisher.

Ten Speed Press
P.O. Box 7123
Berkeley, California 94707
www.tenspeed.com

Distributed in Australia by Simon & Schuster Australia, in
Canada by Ten Speed Press Canada, in New Zealand by
Southern Publishers Group, in South Africa by Real Books,
in Southeast Asia by Berkeley Books, and in the United
Kingdom and Europe by Airlift Book Company.

Cover and book design by Catherine Jacobes
Copyediting by Rebecca Pepper

Library of Congress Cataloging-in-Publication Data

DeMers, John, 1952–
New Orleans by the bowl : gumbos, jambalayas, soups, and
stews / John DeMers with Andrew Jaeger.
    p. cm.
  ISBN 1-58008-324-2
1. Cookery, American—Louisiana style. 2. Cookery—
Louisiana—New Orleans. 3. Stews—Louisiana—New
Orleans. 4. Soups—Louisiana—New Orleans. I. Jaeger,
Andrew. II. Title.
  TX715.2.L68 D47 2003
  641.59763'15—dc21
                                     2002013664

Printed in Canada
First printing, 2003
1 2 3 4 5 6 7 8 9 10 — 07 06 05 04 03

Contents

To all the generations who decided
over three centuries that New Orleans
tasted best when served in a bowl.

Acknowledgments

This book would not have been made possible, or anywhere near as authentic, without my good friend Andrew Jaeger, New Orleans chef. Having grown up above the seafood restaurant his family ran for forty-five years, Andrew has always pointed me to what he calls "the real deal." In a world of culinary artifice and considerable posing in high white hats, finding the real deal in a New Orleans kitchen is a blessing indeed.

Thanks are also due to Andrew's restaurant team: his daughter Mary, Rhoda Yawn, chef Donald James, and Rebecca Collins. Gratitude also goes out to the other great Louisiana chefs who link one tradition to the next and to the one after that, and whose names appear in these pages attached to the traditional recipes they largely made their own: Warren LeRuth, Austin Leslie, Paul Prudhomme, and Paul's talented sister Enola.

For help pulling the many pieces of this book together, Andrew and I would like to thank food writer Rhonda Findley. At Ten Speed Press, we would like to thank Philip Wood, Dennis Hayes, and Brie Mazurek for shepherding this project through many phases and, of course, more than a few bowls.

Introduction

Cooking food for one another has got to be the most realistic thing we do, linking what we need to live, what we want to taste, and what we can get our hands on. Still, I think, for more than three hundred years, New Orleans cooks have been competing for some kind of All-Time Food Realism Award. After paging through this book, you'll probably agree that nobody else ever had a chance.

There have been times in New Orleans' history when virtually no food was to be had—spurring inhabitants to search for edible things that no one thought of eating before. By this point, there aren't too many plants or creatures in south Louisiana's swamps, bayous, bays, forests, or skies that someone hasn't tried hauling into the kitchen. There have been other times when there was plenty of food but not many could afford it. The result was similar—an adventure in creative scavenging, mixed with a general tendency to "stretch" main ingredients by cooking them for a long time in lots of gravy and serving them over lots of rice. Time and again in these pages, you'll see that savvy technique at work and play: buy something that tends to be cheap, tough, and/or tasteless; cook it until it's great, thanks to vegetables and spices; then spoon, ladle, pour, or dump it over mountains of your favorite starch.

Of course, there have also been times when there was plenty of food and plenty of money to buy it, high times based on the riches of cotton or sugar before the Civil War or on oil in the 1970s, before the price per barrel caved in. In such times, the food of New Orleans gets more expensive, more excessive, and far less interesting. Two roast quails per person, instead of one cooked in spicy gravy to feed a family of six. Two classic sauces spooned over one piece of fish or meat, instead of every piece of fish or meat slow-cooked in one huge pot of sauce. Not to sound hopelessly cheap, but I think our food gets boring whenever we strike it rich. Or at least it *would* get boring, if even the richest among us didn't actually prefer to eat poor. In other words, *New Orleans by the Bowl* is all about poor people's food. Just don't try telling the richest people in New Orleans they can't eat it anymore!

A City by the Bowl

Like most of the foods ladled into bowls in its neighborhoods, rich and poor, New Orleans has been about assimilation from the start. There's something about the austerity, the dizzying survival demands, of building a colony on a less-than-desirable piece of New World real estate that enforces pragmatic cooperation, if not always affectionate embrace. As with all those foods in all those bowls, many old cultures have gone into the New Orleans pot. One new culture has come out.

To understand New Orleans "bowl cuisine," it's necessary to grapple with the birthrights of many nations, many histories, and many languages. Ours is an immigrant culture, after all. Yet even issuing the standard pronouncement that New Orleans is "Creole"—meaning French, Spanish, and African—ignores the fact that our most meaningful links are not to the gentle courts of Europe but to the tangled jungles of West Africa and the Middle Passage melting pots of the Caribbean. Despite our quasi-European posturing, you'll find something of Europe in New Orleans but virtually nothing of New Orleans in Europe. Our culture sees its reflection not in the mirrors of Versailles but in the clear, blue waters plied by traders, conquerors, embezzlers, refugees, indentured servants, and slaves.

Still, even before French was spoken here, a colonization beginning in 1718, these bayous, forests, and fields *were* inhabited. Native Americans lived, worked, and cooked here, the same "noble savages" who so fascinated Europeans of the eighteenth century, not to mention the single American who had the most to do with making New Orleans and the rest of the Louisiana Purchase part of the United States, Thomas Jefferson.

Moments of understanding, let alone genuine respect, were few when it comes to these Native Americans, whose tribal affiliations included Choctaw, Attakapas, and Houma. Yet in a strange, New Orleans spin on that fabled first Thanksgiving, the "Indians" were always among us. In 1722, in what historians have nicknamed the Petticoat Rebellion, the women of this struggling French colony marched on Governor Bienville's mansion to protest their altogether boring diet. The governor jumped from both frying pan and fire by hooking the ladies up with his own cook, one Madame Langlois, who shared the secrets she'd learned about hominy and the savory ground sassafras leaves called filé. She'd learned these secrets not from French chefs—there weren't any chefs in France until a bit later anyway—but from men and women of the tribes on the north shore of Lake Pontchartrain. Years later, the French would encounter yet another food tradition in south Louisiana's countryside, an Attakapas smothered corn dish. They tried their best to spell the Native American name, coming up with the pidgin-French words *maque choux*.

The French of New Orleans form the oldest of the city's many immigrations, beginning with the claiming of this bend in the Mississippi for King Louis in 1699 and its clearing for settlement by Jean Baptiste Le Moyne, Sieur de Bienville in the spring of 1718. Still, the French domination was by no means swift, with colonists arriving in several distinct (and now intriguing) waves. Acadians—we know them as Cajuns—were among the first French speakers to disembark, driven from their homes in Nova Scotia between 1756 and 1765 after their defeat by the English in the French and Indian War. The Cajuns, however, generally

rejected life in the "big city" and headed down the Mississippi and its many tributaries toward the Gulf of Mexico—or out onto the broad grasslands of southwest Louisiana, where they would later master the science of growing rice. Cajuns didn't find much to like about New Orleans until the early twentieth century, when the discovery of oil forced them into big business with both New Orleans and their neighbors across the Sabine River in Texas.

Those French who did prefer city life came as a result of several key historical events in France and the French-speaking parts of the New World. The French Revolution of 1789 sent many members of the titled class who escaped the guillotine to this French outpost, a place from which few ever managed to escape. Yet an even more important milestone was the arrival of French-speaking people, both black and white, from the bloodbath of slave rebellions throughout the 1790s on Saint-Domingue, known today as Haiti. These islanders nearly doubled the population of New Orleans, so the fact that their "French" culture was colored with the Catholic-tinged nature worship known as voodoo and infectious rhythms and harmonies from Africa had a dramatic impact on a culture suddenly far removed from Paris. One final flourish of Frenchness happened after New Orleans had (reluctantly) joined the United States. Some of Napoleon

Bonaparte's officers and foot soldiers arrived here after the emperor abdicated the French throne for exile on the remote island of Elba. Around the Napoleon House, a legendary saloon in the French Quarter, these soldiers awaited their general's return to power as long as he was alive.

The Spanish reign in New Orleans proved far less extended than the French—and far less welcome as well. When Louis XV unexpectedly handed the neglected colony to his cousin, Charles III of Spain, on November 3, 1762, there was rebellion, resistance, rioting in the streets—just the sort of thing some visitors enjoy when they come to New Orleans now. The violence got so serious that an Irishman serving Spain (known to history as Don Alejandro O'Reilly) showed up with 1 frigate, 28 transport ships, and 4,900 armed men. Suddenly, the local citizenry recognized the good sense of the ownership change.

It is said, looking back, that the Spanish government taught even French New Orleans new lessons in corruption. All the same, Louisiana history has shown time and again that corruption and effectiveness are not mutually exclusive. Thanks to able governors whose names now inscribe New Orleans streets—most notably Galvez but also Carondolet, Miro, Gayoso, and Salcedo—the Spanish rebuilt what is still called the French Quarter after a disastrous fire, leading the place to have far more in common with Old San Juan than with any city in France. They also rebuilt many aspects of New Orleans cuisine, bringing the rice of paella from Moorish Andalusian kitchens, a dish that evolved into jambalaya. They brought their black beans served over white rice (colorfully called *moros y cristianos*), which evolved into red beans and rice. And they even brought their notion that among the things used to "stretch" dark roasted coffee, toasted and ground chicory root tasted best. If the French delivered the Old World to the doorstep of New Orleans cooking, Spain propelled the Hispanic New World deep into its heart.

The stories of French and Spanish culture in New Orleans have been told and retold throughout the early American history of New Orleans, a function of locals assuring each other how unique they are. But the stories of African culture in New Orleans went underrecognized for some two centuries. Bitterness born of larger racial issues helped agitate what, in some ways, was the country's most tolerant racial climate. As early as 1720, there were free African Americans living in New Orleans; these "Creoles of color" or *gens de couleur libre* numbered nearly 11,000 by the start of the Civil War. Although there were tensions, there was also the recognition that the French language and the Catholic faith helped bind people who otherwise would have been isolated. Many of those who called themselves Creoles competed well in trades like carpentry, cabinetry, and especially masonry, while others grew wealthy and philanthropic. Thomy Lafon, for instance, built hospitals and orphanages with his money, while Henriette de Lille walked away from hers to found an order of nuns ministering to slaves.

Later, after the social upheavals of war and Reconstruction, it was a different type of African American in a different setting who crossed the boundaries between black and white. It was musicians playing a new form of music they called jazz who became the toast of first the short-lived Storyville red-light district and later of New York, Chicago, London, and Paris. Sidney Bechet left New Orleans for Paris and spent more time with Josephine Baker than with most of his kin back home. Louis Armstrong, of the gravel voice and the ingratiating grin, became the best-known ambassador New Orleans ever had. His favorite food, he told anyone who asked, was identified in the way he signed his letters: Red Beans and Ricely Yours.

For a long time, what recognition did reach the African-American cooks of New Orleans reflected their degrees of servitude. The recipes, went the story, were French and Spanish, but all the cooks were African American. Thus, in time, it was only natural that they tweaked this dish or stroked that one. What took much longer to catch on was the truth of a profound African influence, passing from the tribal dishes of that faraway shore through island after island in the Caribbean and finally moving onto the North American continent. This influence has everything to do with *New Orleans by the Bowl,* since innumerable slow-cooked gumbos, stews, and soups that strike onlookers as "soul food" (from gumbo itself to greens stewed with salt pork to smothered black-eyed peas) have linguistic links and even culinary counterparts not in Paris or Madrid but in the villages of West Africa.

As you can see, no single culture made New Orleans food what it is, but a strange, poorly defined, and probably unrepeatable sequence of accidental interactions. These interactions did not stop with French, Spanish, and African influences, however—far from it. The great age of immigration found many landing here and contributing to the melting pot of New Orleans. This century-long assault on any notions of cultural purity was led by Germans, Irish, and Italians and was expanded almost daily by immigrants from Greece, the Dalmatian coast of Croatia, and virtually anywhere that followers of Judaism tried to find or make a home.

Germans were, surprisingly, among the earliest settlers, heeding the invitations of those seeking in vain to lure Frenchmen to Louisiana. As many French arrivals were prisoners, smugglers, and army deserters, the population didn't seem to be heading in a promising direction. With a history of religious and political persecution, though, many Germans thought the promises made in Europe by scoundrels like John Law (who floated the Mississippi Bubble, the first great American real estate scam) sounded like an improvement. Many Germans found their way to the river parishes above New Orleans, an area that became known as the German Coast. This initial colonization is somewhat forgotten, thanks to their habit of blending with the French population. The surname Zweig, for instance, meant twig or branch, filling the records of future generations with citizens renamed LaBranche.

A later wave of Germans remained truer to their homeland, establishing in New Orleans a series of huge, successful beer gardens and restaurants (including the much-missed Kolb's on St. Charles Avenue) and upwards of a dozen first-rate breweries to keep these thirsty places supplied. Still other Germans operated small groceries, with one family building a local chain of stores. Years after these supermarkets shut down, "Schwegmann's" is to groceries in New Orleans what Xerox is to photocopies.

The first Irish, arriving in the early 1700s, were, rather predictably, escapees from a whole series of failed rebellions against British rule. Surely, these people thought, French or Spanish domination would have to be better. Irish immigrants arrived in New Orleans in waves throughout the early nineteenth century, some impoverished, some quite well-to-do. But the floodgates opened in 1845, with the potato famine that reduced Ireland's population by about two million. Even today, a section of New Orleans known as the Irish Channel recalls an unsuccessful effort to keep poor Irish and German settlers from mingling with old-money Creoles of the French Quarter or nouveau riche Americans living on the uptown side of broad Canal Street. The Irish of New Orleans cooked meals, to be sure—the same corned beef and cabbage, Irish stew, and brown bread found in other Irish-heavy cities like Boston. But the legendary Owen Brennan called his restaurant "French" for a reason. As his sister, matriarch Ella Brennan of Commander's Palace, later put it, "There's no such thing as Irish cuisine."

Italians were part of local history as early as 1682, when Henri La Tonti served as LaSalle's lieutenant during his exploration of the Mississippi, but most of the first real settlers disappeared in much the same way that their German counterparts did. Geronimo Chiapella became Gerone La Chapelle, and Filipo Ravenna became Philippe Ravenne. Yet beginning in the mid-1800s, the same immigration from poor, persecuted Sicily and southern Italy that created Little Italys in northern cities like New York gave the New Orleans concept of "Creole" yet another chance to assimilate and expand. Some of the first Italians to arrive became produce farmers on the West Bank of the Mississippi, slowly taking on the task of delivering their goods for sale in New Orleans and eventually expanding the French Market to one of the nation's most colorful produce markets. Restaurants too found their way into the Italian vision, with red sauces made slowly with fresh tomatoes becoming so common they'd later be treated as another invention of the Creoles.

One invention no one could beg, borrow, or steal from the Italians was the muffaletta sandwich, a mountain of cold meats and cheeses laced with savory olive salad on a thick, crusty, round Sicilian loaf. It was created as nourishment for Italian laborers in the market; now visitors from all over the world have to try a muffaletta before they leave New Orleans.

Statistically speaking, these were the major ethnic groups that made the city's culinary mix look and taste like nothing the world had ever seen before. But others have come to the city much as these larger groups did so long ago. Oystermen of the Dalmatian coast came here in the late 1800s, and to this day most of the people supplying our beloved bivalves have names ending in "-ich." Greek sailors stepping off boats at the Mississippi River docks in the middle of that same century stayed, married, founded a church—and became the first official Greek community in the Americas. Jews escaping from Europe came here too, mostly from the Mediterranean branch known as Sephardic. They brought their culture and their tradition of philanthropy, as evidenced by the namesake hospital and other legacies of Judah Touro. And as recently as the 1970s, refugees from war-torn Vietnam made their way to New Orleans, forming Little Saigons at the city's swampy eastern limits as well as on the West Bank.

As has been common among immigrant group after immigrant group for all of New Orleans history, these Vietnamese lived for years at the rumpled fringe of the city's life. Now the young Vietnamese speak English. They want, mostly, what their American friends want. And they eat, mostly, what their American friends eat. Except that, in some mysterious but irreversible way, what we all eat here in New Orleans has been transformed, just a little, once again.

Bowl Cooking Essentials

Bowl cooking has come a long way from its roots, but it still reflects the major inspirations of French, Spanish, and African cuisines. These cultures and more settled in New Orleans, as well as along the bayous of southwest Louisiana. They hunted, fished, and farmed, lived and died, and most of all, ate and drank. Here are the six essential elements of the new cuisine they created.

Rice

South Louisiana wasn't the first place in America to grow rice successfully, but it certainly made the most of it. Once the Carolinas had a great rice culture going in the 1700s, some smart guys realized that the low flatlands now known as Cajun Country could grow rice too. Even better, they figured out more than a century later, these lands were firm enough to support farm machinery as well. It was planting and harvesting machines that turned Louisiana into one of America's (and even the world's) significant sources of rice. In the kitchen, the value of rice to pot cooking is no big secret: it tastes good, it "stretches" anything with a little gravy or sauce thrown in, and it's cheap. No question about it: New Orleans is a meat-and-rice kind of place. Rice is by far the starch of choice in Creole and especially Cajun cooking.

Pasta

After rice, New Orleans cooks have always loved pasta best. Sure, we didn't call it pasta in the old days. Lots of folks just called it spaghetti, no matter what shape of pasta they were using. Even before all those "New Cajun" chefs were demonstrating pasta with crawfish and tasso on national television, the Sicilians were eating spaghetti and oysters. And since they knew where to go for food that tasted real good, the Germans were eating it too. Pasta is a great addition to the New Orleans table.

Seafood

New Orleans is a seafood town. From the city's earliest days, it was easier to get a good meal from the Gulf of Mexico, from the bays and lakes that connect like a jigsaw puzzle across the state's southern wetlands, and of course from all those bayous than to raise most meat or, most expensive of all, have it shipped in. The main seafoods of New Orleans—which, fortunately, have different seasons to keep just about the whole year covered—include fish (redfish, pompano, speckled trout, and flounder are local favorites, though I've been known to fry a croaker or two), shrimp, oysters, crabs, and crawfish. Best of all, since we prefer never to be without something really good, the vast majority of New Orleans dishes famous with one kind of seafood can be cooked with all the other kinds too.

Pork

Of course, we do love a good steak in New Orleans. And we eat a fair amount of chicken too. Even lamb, though definitely not a local thing, is loved by a lot of folks here. But this is the Deep South, and the Deep South is all about pork. Sure, that can mean pork tenderloin, the stuff they now call the "other white meat." But for most of us who grew up here, the fanciest pork we ate was pork chops. Personally, I think pork chops and garlic are one of those marriages made in heaven. However, the main role of pork in south Louisiana is expressed with two S's: sausage and seasoning. Here, pork becomes smoked sausage that will knock your socks off, the most famous being known by the French word for several traditional forms of sausage, andouille. It also can become tasso, a salty, spicy ham that should be used in small amounts to add intriguing flavor. And finally, all kinds of cheap pork cuts have been used for generations to add taste to stews, vegetables such as turnip or mustard greens, and—best of all—red beans.

The Trinity

New Orleans can be an amazingly religious place, although most of the tourists on Bourbon Street would never guess it. But in the kitchen, references to the Trinity or even the Holy Trinity are not to any Catholic teaching but to the three "divine" ingredients that start off virtually every local dish: onion, bell pepper, and celery. Just about any dish worth eating in New Orleans starts with a chopped-up pile of those vegetables—sometimes called simply "seasoning." Even dishes that are going to simmer for hours start with a sauté of that trinity, since we like the special sweetness that happens when you sizzle onion, bell pepper, and celery in a little oil or butter. The world is full of shortcuts, but skipping this step is considered, well, a mortal sin.

Seasoning Mixes and Pepper Sauces

Creole and Cajun dishes don't have to burn your mouth. As the old pot cooks used to put it, the idea was to season everything "just right." Still, we New Orleanians do like things with a little kick, an element that usually comes in with one or both of two now-common products. I think every kitchen should have a shaker of Creole or Cajun seasoning, and you have a ton of them to choose from. You'll need to taste some to decide which you prefer, but you can start by reading labels. Most seasoning blends are primarily salt—and, unless you have doctor's orders to obey, there's nothing wrong with that. It's the proportions of all the other herbs and spices (including cayenne pepper for heat) that'll help you decide which blend is your favorite. You can also make your own seasoning mix. The recipe on page 34 is a good starting point.

You'll need to use the same taste test to choose from all the Louisiana hot sauces on the shelf. There used to be only one that was widely available—Tabasco, from Avery Island near New Iberia—but now the list goes on and on. Crystal from New Orleans makes some good sauces, as do Louisiana Gold and Panola.

New Orleans Glossary

Andouille [ahn-DWEE]: Here we have a French tradition that made a run for the pepper when it arrived in south Louisiana. In other words, you will find the word *andouille* in France, but you won't find the flavor. This is the smoked sausage used to season red beans and rice, and it's also grilled or pan-fried in long slices to be served on a po' boy.

Bell pepper: Creole and Cajun dishes get a kind of sweet, vegetable background flavor from the fact that these "sweet peppers" (as opposed to hot peppers) are added to the onions and celery. For color, we suppose it's okay if you mix green bells with the now-popular red and yellow ones. But green is always preferred for the deep, soulful flavors of New Orleans pot cooking.

Bisque [bihsk]: In classical French cooking, a bisque is a thick and usually puréed cream soup, and these are still found around New Orleans as shrimp bisque or, more sophisticatedly, lobster bisque. But what separates our bisque from everybody else's is crawfish bisque, a time-honored (and time-consuming) dish that involves cleaning out crawfish shells and refilling them with a stuffing of picked tail meat and seasoned bread crumbs. When a New Orleanian serves you homemade crawfish bisque, he or she likes you a lot.

Blackened: As best we can tell, Cajuns weren't blackening redfish on the bayou three hundred years ago. If they had been, from the way things have gone since the 1980s, there wouldn't be any redfish left to blacken. With the redfish population now protected and returning to good health, we can again enjoy this strange cooking technique. The secrets to blackening include covering the fish (or meat or whatever) with Cajun spices and searing it in a really hot dry skillet. This seals in the juices. Don't try this inside if you have a smoke alarm!

Blue crab: Hard-shell or soft-shell, blue crabs are the favorite in the crab capital of the Deep South. Most vacations along the Gulf, in fact, include dropping a line with a chicken neck or other goodie into the water and pulling up crabs that latch on day and night. Backfin or jumbo lump crabmeat is the most esteemed from among the picked crabmeat available in supermarkets.

Soft-shell crabs, taken when one hard shell falls off and another one hasn't quite hardened yet, are a local specialty, whether sautéed and served with a side of creamy pasta or batter-fried for enjoyment on a po' boy.

Bouillabaisse [BOOL-yuh-BAYZ]: According to some local food historians, this seafood stew beloved in the town of Marseilles is the ancient basis for Louisiana gumbo. But the differences between the two stews are more profound than the similarities, bouillabaisse being a delicate, brothy seafood concoction with a few tomatoes and a hint of saffron, and gumbo being a bold, dark statement thickened by roux and kicked up by hot peppers.

Café au lait: Literally "milk coffee," this favored beverage has an almost religious hold on the coffee drinkers of New Orleans. For one thing, it's got to be made with French dark roast coffee (not black like espresso, but getting close). For another thing, most locals like their coffee brewed with chicory, the ground-up and roasted cousin of Belgian endive that imparts a bitterness New Orleanians find pleasant. The milk has to be heated just until scalding, then poured into the cup simultaneously with the almost thick, dark coffee. It's quite a ceremony, but it sure is good.

Cajun: Cajun is a shorter, mispronounced version of the French word *Acadien,* meaning anyone who came to Louisiana from what we now call Nova Scotia as part of the British occupation. In general, Cajun cooking is country cooking producing immense flavors by putting everything in sight into a single (usually cast-iron) pot and cooking the mixture for a long time. The prime component is *not* hot peppers or hot pepper sauce, though many an airport eatery a thousand miles away have made it seem so. Restaurants have added subtle layerings in recent years, but traditional Cajun dishes still draw their appeal from slow, careful cooking and what Cajun cooks universally describe as "a lotta love."

Cayenne pepper: This ground red pepper remains the primary source of "hot" in hot Creole and Cajun. At crawfish boils, for instance, boilers try to outdo one another in the amount of cayenne they can dump into the heat-swirled waters. Still, if you seek some form of New Orleans authenticity, remember that "hot" isn't really what Creole or Cajun food is all about. It's about being "well seasoned," which means kissed with a balance of different herbs and spices.

Court-bouillon [koor-bwee-YAHN]: In France, a court-bouillon is a "short broth," a quick little stock to be used in cooking something else. In New Orleans, however, a court-bouillon is a bigger production: a fish or other main ingredient is slowly cooked in a light sauce given color and a little body by the addition of tomatoes. Redfish or sea bass are the fish of choice.

Crawfish: You can call these mudbugs "crayfish" all you want, but that won't be what they are. Everybody around New Orleans knows they're crawfish, the darling of backyard crawfish boils throughout the spring crawfish season. Most of the best "wild" crawfish come from the Atchafalaya Basin west of Baton Rouge, but increasingly the crawfish we get are farmed in flooded rice fields. So the same field may give us both the crawfish for the étouffée and the rice we'll happily spoon it over.

Creole: In New Orleans, Creole indicates a broad mixture of cultures from the Caribbean to the far-flung islands of the Indian Ocean. Despite several decades of blending with Cajun cooking in New Orleans restaurant recipes, Creole cooking is city cooking for the most part, often with French, Spanish, and African influences—a cuisine of the vibrant markets in a busy port city. Creole cooking is more likely than Cajun to be based on classical French method, with greater importance on butter and cream, and separate sauces prepared for serving over meats and seafoods.

Creole mustard: Eat your heart out, Dijon. Sometime back in the mists of local history, New Orleanians decided they like a coarse-grain mustard that clears out the sinuses as though it were horseradish. German immigrants actually brought the first mustard seeds to the area from Austria and Holland, right along with the signature process that gives our mustard its unique flavor—steeping the seeds in vinegar. Creole mustard is great on a ham sandwich, but it's even greater in one or more Creole sauces, including the one called rémoulade that is spooned over shrimp.

Étouffée [ay-too-FAY]: The word in French is simple enough, meaning "smothered," a reference to being cooked in a pan with the lid on. But that only starts the tale of étouffée in south Louisiana, an almost holy word applied most often to crawfish but sometimes to shrimp or chicken. Crawfish étouffée is a crawfish stew slow-cooked in a mixture of sauce and roux. The finished product can range from red to brown, but it is never allowed to range too far from delicious.

Filé [FEE-lay]: This powder is made from ground sassafras leaves. If the earliest French explorers hadn't gone looking for survival tips from the American Indians already living on the north shore of Lake Pontchartrain, we might not have filé or filé gumbo today. The powder adds flavor to any liquid, but mostly it serves as a thickening agent. Don't add it to your gumbo until it's been removed from the heat, and don't use filé in gumbo already thickened by okra. If you do, you might find yourself using the gumbo as mortar between bricks.

Grillade [gree-YAHD]: Before there was a meal known officially as brunch and celebrated in New Orleans with cocktails and maybe a few glasses of wine, there was "second breakfast"—a late-morning repast enjoyed by early-rising French Market vendors after they knocked off for the day. A favorite dish at second breakfast was this lightly spicy, red-saucy, slow-cooked beef or veal dish, invariably served with a side of buttery grits.

Gumbo: Although New Orleans is both French and Spanish, you'll never find anything that looks or tastes like gumbo in France or Spain. We laugh when someone says it's like the bouillabaisse of Marseilles, a fine enough soup to be sure, but light and subtle and unexciting by comparison. Gumbo takes its name from the African word for okra, the use of okra to thicken soup being one of culinary history's true turning points. Everybody's mama makes the world's best gumbo, but you can make it with any seafood, with chicken and andouille sausage (sometimes called gumbo ya-ya), or just with vegetables. A vegetarian version called gumbo z'herbes in the old Creole patois is a Lenten favorite in ever-Catholic New Orleans.

Gumbo crabs: Not so much a type of crab (like Alaskan King or Dungeness) as a size, gumbo crab is any crab that strikes the cook as just right for making gumbo. Like the choice of so many ingredients in New Orleans cooking, the choice of crabs for gumbo was originally a process of elimination. Seafood mongers sold off all the crabs anybody wanted to boil, whether for instant consumption or for picking out the delicate meat; what was leftover got used in gumbo. These crabs were small, making for much labor per ounce of crabmeat, so it was far better to boil them in gumbo and let the diner pick out the tiny pockets of meat. Gumbo novices, beware the claws!

Jambalaya: No one knows for sure how jambalaya got its name, but we love the story that it's based on something a hungry Frenchman told his cook named Jean late at night, "Jean, belayez." Or, "Jean, throw something together." Jambalaya, however it got its name, is Louisiana paella—a rice dish, probably Spanish-inspired, filled with seafood, chicken, sausage, and who knows what else. Little wars are fought between cooks who like "red jambalaya" with tomatoes and those who like "brown jambalaya" without tomatoes. Either way, it's a great excuse to clean all the leftovers out of your refrigerator.

Louisiana hot sauce: These days, even the blandest grocery store features a whole section of hot sauces—including dozens from the habanero-crazed Hispanic sector, some from the Caribbean and Africa, and maybe even a few from Southeast Asia. But thanks to a place near New Iberia called Avery Island, Louisiana is ground zero for hot sauces. Avery Island is where globe-trotting Tabasco comes from, produced by the McIlhenny family for nearly a century and a half and still one of America's best-recognized trademarks.

Maque choux [MAHK shoo]: The name of this dish might look French, but it's not. It's merely a name French explorers and colonists slapped on what they thought they heard the local Indians saying. In other words, the *choux* in "maque choux" has nothing to do with cabbage. Maque choux is a corn dish (oftentimes cooked almost to mush, like a corn pudding), given extra flavor by tomatoes, onions, and green bell peppers. Old-fashioned Creole and Cajun cooks used to "milk" the ears with a sharp knife and incorporate the liquid into the dish. Today, a dash of whole milk or even cream can hit the spot.

Mirliton [MER-lih-ton]: If you've never heard of mirlitons, then maybe you've heard of "vegetable pear" or at least the Hispanic chayote. These are all names for the same thing, a tart, hard, squashlike fruit that grows in many people's backyards around New Orleans. As such, it's not surprising that so many favorite dishes cooked by mothers and grandmothers feature mirlitons. They are generally stuffed and baked in the same way as eggplant and bell peppers.

Muffaletta [moof-fuh-LEHT-tuh]: The Sicilian sandwich to end all Sicilian sandwiches, muffaletta got its name from the bread it rode in on—a crusty round loaf favored by Sicilians working in the French Market. In the beginning, these men bought the muffaletta loaf and piled it high with cold cuts, cheeses, and a savory olive salad. Eventually, the people selling the bread and fillings discovered they could charge more by selling the whole sandwich. A Sicilian star was born.

Okra: Okra is grown in many parts of the world today, but by all accounts, it came to New Orleans from Africa. It is a bizarre green pod with edible flesh and seeds inside, not to mention a kind of sticky, clear juice that thickens gumbo and other stews as the okra cooks down. The word *gumbo* means "okra" in one of the West African tribal languages. In addition to using okra in soups and stews, we love okra that's been fried.

Oysters: Oysters live and are consumed in lots of coastal areas around the United States (and even around the world). Suffice it to say that in south Louisiana, south Louisiana oysters are considered the finest, freshest, and saltiest on the face of the earth. In a tribute to the area's role as melting pot, the oyster industry has long been dominated by immigrants from Croatia, that fiercely proud section of the former Yugoslavia. Oysters are enjoyed raw on the half shell, with a squeeze of lemon and a splash of Tabasco, or they can be used in any number of gumbos, soups, and stews.

Oyster water: It is quite common around New Orleans to see recipes call for "oyster water" or "oyster liquor." Both phrases refer to the liquid captured inside the oyster shell, which runs out when you start shucking. The oyster flavor contained in this liquid is mild but noticeable, making oyster water a desirable addition to any oyster dish. The trick is capturing the stuff. One clear-cut method is to shuck oysters over a tray or shallow bowl. But be sure to strain the liquid before use, or plenty of dust, grit, and oyster shell will muddy up the precious juice. If you don't want to get your hands dirty, you can substitute clam juice.

Pain perdu [pan pehr-DOO]: The old Creoles had a knack for giving their favorite foods colorful names, and this is one of the most colorful. This variation on French toast is more than French enough, giving New Orleans cooks a chance to use up French bread bought yesterday and now too dry to eat. As this stale bread could be considered "lost," the recipe that brought it back to life was found—and named *pain perdu,* "lost bread."

Pickled pork: If you've never heard of this seasoning meat, then you're definitely not from Louisiana.

Traditionally, most recipes for this pig shoulder marinated in brine involve a difficult process of stretching the meat over two weeks. Today, pickled pork is produced commercially and sold in meat markets and even grocery stores. It can be used to flavor almost anything, but it's especially beloved in red beans and rice. If you can't find pickled pork, the best substitute is ham or ham hock, preferably one that's been dry cured—that is, heavily salted and allowed to absorb the salt over a duration of time.

Pralines: Please, it's never "pray-leens," always "praw-leens." These are the candies extraordinaire of New Orleans, in the past sold from baskets by bandanaed women who strolled through the French Quarter calling out their sweet wares. Today, most pralines are made by a handful of companies. They are simple enough to make in your own kitchen; just show a bit of care with the sugar temperatures (true of any candymaking) and you'll have a pecan praline to be proud of in no time.

Red beans: Poor people all over the world subsist on some version of rice and beans. The type of bean varies, reflecting the geography and the ethnicity doing the subsisting. In New Orleans, no question, hands down, day in and day out, our bean is the red bean. The red kidney bean, to be precise. There can be other uses, but it wouldn't come as a surprise if 98 or 99 percent of the red beans enjoyed in New Orleans are enjoyed as red beans and rice, maybe with a big piece of smoked andouille on the side.

Roux [ROO]: A traditional French method of thickening soups and stews, the roux of south Louisiana has traveled a long way from the old country. Ranging from beige to almost black, this thick base is a mixture of fat (butter, oil, or lard) and flour that has been cooked until the taste of flour is gone. Roux is the cornerstone of many Canjun and Creole bowl dishes.

Tasso [TAH-soh]: Before the Cajun invasion of the early 1980s, most New Orleanians had heard as much about tasso as folks on Michigan's Upper Peninsula had. All that has changed, however, with this Cajun pork product now welcomed into both Creole and Cajun dishes. Tasso is also never eaten on its own—it's too smoky and salty for most people to enjoy that. But it is unchallenged in the ability of a tiny piece to give intense yet complex flavor to beans, soups, crawfish dishes, and silky cream sauces spooned over pasta.

Trinity: This seasoning mix—chopped onions, bell pepper, and celery—is at the heart of almost every Creole and Cajun dish. Some cooks insist that the three vegetables be represented in equal amounts, while others give pride of place to the onions. All we know is that cooking with the Trinity gives us all a great reason to count our blessings.

Yams: Louisiana really loves yams—except that they aren't really yams. For those bland and starchy tubers, look to the Caribbean and Latin America. The produce item sold all over the world as a "Louisiana yam" is actually a sweet potato. And of course, because no tradition cooks sweet potatoes for side dishes or desserts better than the African-American one, they've found a special place on the New Orleans menu. A recently developed favorite pairs sweet potatoes with a sauce of brown sugar and pecans.

Basics

THE BUILDING BLOCKS OF NEW ORLEANS GUMBOS and other bowl dishes are fairly simple, but perfecting them can take a whole lot of bowls. Once you master the principles of making roux, stocks, and seasoning, the trick is then to add your personal flair. This chapter offers some basics for making the recipes in the book and for getting started on your own Creole creations.

Roux

There can be no question: the single element that makes gumbos, étouffées, soups, and stews taste like they're from New Orleans is roux—that dramatic (if careful) blending of flour and fat to form a deep-brown, nutty-tasting, soul-satisfying sauce thickener. Of course, no two Creole or Cajun cooks make roux exactly alike. Some make it at the beginning of a dish and build out from there, following the age-old dictate of New Orleans mamas to their daughters, "First you make a roux." Others prepare the roux near the end, incorporating it according to the needs of all that's happened in the pot so far. You'll find that the recipes in this book are similarly varied—though most do start with a roux.

The basics of roux making are easy enough to grasp. The art and science of roux making, however, will demand a lifetime. Still, no other element will sign your name among the greats of New Orleans cooking with quite the same flourish as turning out a terrific roux.

People who live in New Orleans think of roux as being dark brown, because that's the color used to thicken most of our famous gumbos and étouffées. Yet a roux can be any mix of equal parts flour and fat ranging in color from nearly white (sometimes called "blond roux," cooked barely long enough for the flour to lose its raw taste) through medium brown (also known as peanut butter roux) to a brown that verges on black, like espresso coffee grounds. The goal of most cooks is to take the roux to the brink, to push it almost to burning yet never let it burn. Like bullfighters working close to the horns, they stand at their skillets, stirring and assessing until the last possible moment before the fire department rushes in. Roux doesn't cost very much to throw out, but the disgrace among New Orleans cooks of doing so is considerable. And some cooks even make too much roux on purpose since you can seal it in a jar and store it in the refrigerator for use as needed.

The pieces of a roux are simple. Most locals prefer a heavy, black, cast-iron skillet, the kind their mothers and grandmothers used—and sometimes even the same one. The heat distribution is quick and even, considered a good thing in virtually all cooking. On the other hand, just about any skillet or sauté pan can make a roux, once you understand and master how it distributes heat. Although you'll see slight variations, flour and oil are normally used in equal amounts. This produces a smooth, almost pasty mixture that then can be browned to your heart's content. To this day, some cooks make their roux using butter instead of oil, a simple preference of taste.

Traditional cooks brown a roux over very low heat, stirring until their elbows are sore. It's a sign of a different time, perhaps, a time when people simply weren't so rushed. The impetus to make roux faster came, not surprisingly, from professional kitchens, where time spent on each dish is crucial to its practicality and profitability. Roux, we now know, can be turned out pretty fast, though no less carefully than the older generations used to make them. Some people have experimented with roux cooked in the oven (in a sense, heat is heat) and even with no fat (browned flour can thicken—but is it a roux?).

One of the most common mistakes of new roux makers—other than getting the hot stuff on their skin; it sizzles like napalm!—is burning the mixture after they think they're finished cooking it. With all the heat in the skillet, merely removing the pan from the burner isn't good enough. The best trick from old Creole cooks is to add chopped onion, bell pepper, celery, and garlic, an assault that will stop the browning almost immediately. If you're really careful to avoid splattering, you can even incorporate some of your gumbo or soup into the roux, stirring until a delicious, deliriously scented sludge develops. Nothing will ever make roux dissolve into your dish easier than adding some of your dish to the roux first.

Stocks

Another basic element that gives New Orleans bowl dishes the taste of authenticity is homemade stock. Making stock is much easier than most modern home cooks think it is. It may seem time-consuming, involving a large pot left bubbling gently on a back burner of your stove for an hour or two or more, but difficult it's not. Making stock from scratch propels you into a timeless tradition of classic cooking, with dozens of possible uses in soups, stews, and sauces.

For our purposes, the production of France's traditional mother sauces is less important than turning out delicious poultry, seafood, or meat broth that adds flavor where plain water would take it away. The making of stock flows from a now nearly-forgotten sequence of kitchen tasks in which birds, fish, and other animals start out with the meat still on the bones, allowing the bones to flavor the water into stock or broth. If you're accustomed to buying boneless meat and precut and frozen vegetables, making stock might prove a bit of a challenge. But when it comes to New Orleans bowl cooking, nothing in a can or jar equals the flavor of a dish made with homemade stock.

Seasoning

Creole and Cajun seasoning are the same thing—nothing more (or less) than someone's favorite blend of all-purpose dry spices. The mix is usually heaviest in salt, generally followed by black and white pepper, cayenne pepper , garlic and onion powder, and paprika for a little color. Some commercial blends are marketed from companies, others are associated with high-profile chefs, and still others are prescribed with near-medical precision for special uses, such as seasoning seafood, beef, or vegetables. As with roux and stocks (and so many other aspects of New Orleans cooking, for that matter), seasoning often involves a bit of improvisation and trial and error to achieve that perfect personal touch that smacks of down-home cooking.

Basic Roux

Many of the recipes in this book treat making the roux as one of their steps, but some call for a pre-made roux. What follows is a basic, multipurpose recipe to make light, medium, or dark brown roux. Light brown roux is generally used to thicken sauces or gravies for heavy beef, venison, and wild game, while medium brown roux lends a stronger, nuttier flavor to pork, veal, and seafood. Dark brown roux is perfect for gumbo and most other classics. In New Orleans and the rest of south Louisiana, if a recipe calls simply for "roux," dark roux is implied.

Creole cooks have a convenient way of stopping roux from cooking past the desired color. After removing the roux from the heat, immediately stir in some chopped seasoning vegetables, such as onion, bell pepper, and celery. The vegetables will stop the roux from getting any darker or burning.

....

Yields 6 cups

3 cups vegetable oil
3 cups all-purpose flour

Heat the oil in a skillet or large saucepot over medium heat until it starts to smoke. Slowly stir in the flour, small batches at a time, making sure to scrape the flour from the bottom of the skillet, since that flour will brown (or even burn) before the flour on top will. Lower the heat to medium-low and cook, stirring, until the desired color is achieved: For a light brown roux, cook until just smooth and light brown, 5 to 7 minutes. For a medium brown roux, cook until a peanut butter color is achieved, 10 to 12 minutes. For dark brown roux, cook until thick and dark brown (almost black without burning), 15 to 18 minutes. Remove the skillet from the heat; be careful, as the roux will be extremely hot. Extra roux can be covered and stored in the refrigerator for up to 2 weeks.

Shrimp Stock

Yields 4 cups

2 pounds shrimp heads and shells (from 6 pounds
   whole shrimp)
8 cups water
1/2 cup chopped onion
1/2 cup chopped green bell pepper
1/2 cup chopped celery
3 bay leaves

Put the shrimp heads and shells in a large stockpot.
Reserve the shrimp for another use. Add the water,
onion, bell pepper, celery, and bay leaves to the
pot with the heads and shells. Bring to a boil over
high heat and continue cooking until the liquid
is reduced by half. Strain, reserving the liquid and
discarding the shells and heads. If not using immediately, store the stock in a sealed container and
refrigerate for 3 to 4 days, or freeze.

Crab Stock

Yields 4 cups

4 pounds whole gumbo crabs
8 cups chopped onion
8 cups chopped celery
8 cups peeled, chopped carrot
6 bay leaves
8 cups water

Wash the crabs. In a large stockpot, crush the crabs
and sauté them over high heat until they turn
orange. Add the chopped vegetables, bay leaves,
and water. Over high heat, bring to a boil and
continue boiling until the liquid is reduced by half.
Strain, reserving only the liquid. Discard the
vegetables and crabs. If not using immediately,
store the stock in a sealed container and refrigerate
for 3 to 4 days, or freeze.

Crawfish Stock

Yields about 4 cups

1/4 cup olive oil

6 carrots, peeled and chopped

4 onions, chopped

3 stalks celery, chopped

2 leeks, both white and green parts, chopped

5 pounds live crawfish

6 cloves garlic, chopped

10 tomatoes, chopped

8 cups water

3 bay leaves

Heat the oil in a stockpot over medium-high heat and sauté the carrots, onions, celery, and leeks. Add the live crawfish along with the garlic, stirring until the crawfish turn bright red. Add the tomatoes, water, and bay leaves; bring to a boil and cook for 20 minutes. Skim any impurities that rise to the top. Strain the stock through a fine sieve. Discard the vegetables and crawfish. If not using immediately, store the stock in a sealed container and refrigerate for 3 to 4 days, or freeze.

Fish Stock

Yields about 4 cups

2 tablespoons olive oil

6 carrots, peeled and chopped

4 onions, chopped

3 stalks celery, chopped

1 leek, both white and green parts, chopped

8 cups water

4 bay leaves

5 pounds fish bones, including heads and tails, gills and blood removed

Heat the oil in a stockpot over medium-high heat and sauté the carrots, onions, celery, and leek until they start to brown. Add the water, bay leaves, and fish bones, bringing the liquid to a boil. Skim any impurities that rise to the top. Strain through a fine sieve. Discard the vegetables and fish bones. If not using immediately, store the stock in a sealed container and refrigerate for 3 to 4 days, or freeze.

Chicken Stock

Yields 8 cups

2 pounds chicken bones
6 quarts water
1 cup peeled, chopped carrot
1/2 cup chopped onion
1/2 cup chopped celery, with leaves
1/2 cup chopped fresh parsley
Pinch of fresh thyme
1 bay leaf
Salt and ground white pepper

Preheat the oven to 400°F. Place the bones in a roasting pan and brown them in the oven for 15 to 20 minutes. Bring the water to a boil over high heat in a large stockpot. Add the browned bones and the remaining ingredients, reduce the heat to medium, and simmer for 1 hour, or until the liquid is reduced by half. Remove the pan from the heat and allow the stock to cool, then refrigerate for 4 to 5 hours. Remove all of the fat that has gathered at the surface of the liquid, then strain the stock with a colander. Discard the bones and vegetables. If not using immediately, store the stock in a sealed container and refrigerate for 3 to 4 days, or freeze.

Beef Stock

Yields 8 cups

10 pounds cut beef bones
2 pounds large carrots
4 large yellow onions, cut in half
2 stalks celery, cut in thirds
1 cup garlic cloves
1 bunch parsley
1 tablespoon black peppercorns
12 quarts water

Preheat the oven to 350°F. Place the bones, carrots, onions, and celery in a large roasting pan. Roast until brown, about 1 hour. Put in a large stockpot and add the remaining ingredients. Bring to a boil. Lower the heat and simmer for 4 to 5 hours, until the stock is dark and just starting to thicken. Add more water if necessary. Strain, retaining the liquid and discarding the other ingredients. Let cool and skim off the fat. If not using immediately, store the stock in a sealed container and refrigerate for 3 to 4 days, or freeze.

Duck Stock

Yields 4 cups

2 tablespoons olive oil

3 onions, chopped

2 carrots, peeled and chopped

6 stalks celery, chopped

10 pounds duck bones

1 tablespoon black peppercorns

4 quarts water

Heat the oil in a large stockpot over medium-high heat and sauté the onions, carrots, and celery for about 3 minutes. Add the duck bones, peppercorns, and water. Lower the heat and simmer for about 3 hours, until the stock is dark and just starting to thicken, skimming off any impurities that rise to the top. Strain through a fine sieve, discarding the bones and vegetables. If not using immediately, store the stock in a sealed container and refrigerate for 3 to 4 days, or freeze.

Venison Stock

Yields 4 quarts

8 pounds deer bones

2 onions, chopped

4 stalks celery, chopped

3 carrots, peeled and chopped

1/2 cup tomato purée

6 quarts water

1 head garlic, peeled and crushed

2 bay leaves

1 tablespoon black peppercorns

Preheat the oven to 400°F. Roast the bones in a roasting pan until browned, about 1 hour. Spread the onions, celery, carrots, and tomato purée on top of the bones and return to the oven for about 20 minutes more. Transfer the roasted bone mixture to a large stockpot and add the water, garlic, bay leaves, and peppercorns. Use a little water to help scrape the browned drippings from the roasting pan, and add them to the stockpot. Bring the liquid to a boil, lower the heat, and simmer for 5 to 6 hours, until the stock is dark and just starting to thicken, skimming off any impurities. Strain the stock through a fine sieve. Discard the bones and vegetables. If not using immediately, store the stock in a sealed container and refrigerate for 3 to 4 days, or freeze.

Creole Seasoning

The following is a versatile, satisfying Creole seasoning with less salt than the norm. You should feel free to tinker with it to turn it into your own personal blend.

....

Yields about ¾ cup

5 tablespoons paprika

1 tablespoon ground black pepper

1 tablespoon ground white pepper

1 tablespoon cayenne pepper

1 tablespoon dried thyme

2 tablespoons garlic powder

1 tablespoon dried oregano

1 teaspoon salt

1 teaspoon chile powder

1 teaspoon onion powder

Blend all ingredients very well. Store in a tightly covered jar.

Gumbos

A STRANGE DISH WITH AN EVEN STRANGER NAME, gumbo is the ultimate New Orleans soup. Or stew. Or seafood dish. Whatever it is, gumbo is the dish most likely to be remembered from the kitchen of your New Orleans mama. (Or daddy, since gumbo is to gender in Louisiana what barbecue is in Texas: a masculine dish when it needs to be.) Either parent can make the gumbo. In fact, sometimes both make the gumbo together. Or each makes his or her own gumbo, creating a friendly rivalry over the stove.

There is the wonderful story about a funeral set among the Cajuns of south Louisiana—a funeral for a man who was horrible to everybody. No one could remember one nice thing he'd ever done, one kind word he'd ever spoken. But now he was dead, and someone had to stand up and say something. "Well," a person who knew him well began, then paused to clear his throat and search for one positive memory. "Well...who's gonna make the gumbo now?" Someone who makes good gumbo is someone you never want to lose.

Like many foundational dishes around the world, gumbo isn't really all that hard to make. Most people start with stock or broth; add meat, chicken, or seafood along with the Holy Trinity (chopped onion, bell pepper, and celery), probably some okra, maybe some smoked sausage, and maybe some tomato (highly controversial but undeniably tasty), and then thicken it with dark roux. You can start with plain water, of course, but why would anybody start with less flavor instead of more? You really can cook gumbo any way you want and add or take away anything you want.

Gumbo, by the way, takes its name from the word for okra in several West African dialects. According to historians, the pod we know as okra made the crossing on the slave ships, perhaps as a last piece of home grabbed up and hidden as the slaves were dragged away. We know that in the slave quarters of south Louisiana plantations, okra was grown around many of the huts and passionately appreciated in dishes cooked over the communal fire. It is entirely fitting that a dish invented by slaves became a dish that helps all the people in New Orleans eat like kings.

Seafood Gumbo

Here is the classic New Orleans seafood gumbo, the kind everybody's mama always makes best. There are actually stories of bachelors waiting to taste their intended's seafood gumbo before deciding whether to pop the question. We're much too enlightened to do such a thing now, of course.

Serves 6 to 8

2 pounds extra-large (16/20) shrimp

6 cups water

1 cup vegetable oil, plus more for sautéing

1 cup all-purpose flour

1/2 pound smoked slab bacon, diced

3/4 pound fresh okra, chopped

4 stalks celery, chopped

2 large onions, chopped

1 bunch green onions, both white and green parts, chopped

4 cloves garlic, chopped

1 green bell pepper, chopped

1 teaspoon dried thyme

2 bay leaves

3 tablespoons chopped parsley

3 tablespoons tomato paste

1 pound fresh crabmeat

Creole seasoning (page 34)

Louisiana hot sauce

3 or 4 cups cooked white rice

Boil the shrimp in the water. When they are pink, drain, cool, peel, and devein, preserving the water as stock.

Make a dark brown roux by stirring 1 cup of the oil and the flour together in a skillet over medium-high heat until a dark brown color is achieved (see page 29).

In a large stew pot, stir the diced bacon over medium heat until it begins to crisp, then remove it from the pot. Sauté the okra in the bacon drippings until it loses all signs of the sliminess that will ultimately let it thicken the gumbo. Add a small amount of vegetable oil, followed by the celery, onions, garlic, bell pepper, thyme, bay leaves, and parsley. Sauté until the vegetables are cooked, about 7 minutes. Add the tomato paste, stirring 1 to 2 minutes more.

Pour in the shrimp stock and return the bacon to the pot. Bring the gumbo to a boil, then thicken it gradually with the roux until a smooth, rich consistency is achieved. Cover the pot and simmer for 1 hour. When ready to serve, return the peeled shrimp to the pot and add the crabmeat. Season to taste with Creole seasoning and hot sauce. Remove and discard the bay leaves. Serve in soup bowls over white rice.

Gumbo Ya-Ya

Somewhere along the way, this inland chicken and andouille gumbo (loved by the Cajuns who live on farms far removed from the bayous and the Gulf) came to be known as Gumbo Ya-Ya. Still, the name sounds Creole to me, with that lyrical twist the Creole cooks applied to all their favorite dishes—even as they made them taste better than they ever had before.

Serves 8

1 (5-pound) hen, cut into 10 pieces

2 teaspoons Creole seasoning
(page 34)

2¹/₂ cups all-purpose flour

1 cup vegetable oil

2 cups chopped onion

1¹/₂ cups chopped celery

2 cups chopped green bell pepper

6 cups chicken stock (page 32)

1¹/₂ teaspoons minced garlic

1 pound andouille or other smoked
sausage, chopped

Salt and ground black pepper

4 cups cooked white rice

About 30 minutes before starting, season the chicken pieces with the Creole seasoning; let stand at room temperature. Place the flour in a large paper bag, add the chicken and shake until well coated. Reserve 1 cup of the flour. Heat the oil in a large skillet over medium-high heat, and brown the chicken on all sides. Remove the chicken and set aside. When cooled, cut the meat from the bones and cut into chunks. Using a wire whisk, stir the skillet to loosen the browned particles from the bottom, then stir in the reserved flour. Stir constantly over medium-high heat until the roux is dark brown (see page 29).

Remove the roux from the heat and add the chopped vegetables, stirring to stop the roux from browning while cooking the vegetables. Transfer this mixture to a large pot, pour in the chicken stock, and bring to a boil. Lower the heat to a simmer, and add the sausage and chicken. Continue cooking for 45 minutes over low heat. Adjust the seasoning with salt and pepper. Serve in soup bowls over white rice.

Smoked Rabbit Gumbo

Smoked just-about-anything will work great in this recipe, but New Orleans cooks (who sometimes are just New Orleans hunters in disguise) love what happens when they have fresh rabbit and a craving for gumbo at the same time

....

Serves 8

2 rabbits, cleaned and cut into
   serving pieces
1/2 cup vegetable oil
1/2 cup all-purpose flour
1 onion, chopped
1 medium green bell pepper, chopped
4 stalks celery, chopped
4 cloves garlic, chopped
2 teaspoons Creole seasoning
   (page 34)
3 bay leaves
8 cups chicken stock (page 32)
5 tablespoons Louisiana hot sauce
1/4 cup Worcestershire sauce
4 cups cooked white rice
Chopped green onion, both white and
   green parts, for garnish

Smoke the rabbit pieces in a home smoker, or place them in a pan and set it atop smoking wood chips. Smoke the rabbit until it is golden brown, then allow it to cool and cut the meat from the bones.

Heat the oil in a sauté pan over medium-high heat, add the flour, and cook, stirring to make a make a dark brown roux (see page 29). Stir in the onion, bell pepper, celery, and garlic and cook until the vegetables are softened, about 10 minutes. Add the Creole seasoning, bay leaves, stock, hot sauce, and Worcestershire sauce. Simmer until the gumbo is dark and thick, about 45 minutes. Remove and discard the bay leaves. Serve in soup bowls over white rice, garnished with green onion.

Turkey and Sausage Gumbo

You can smell this gumbo cooking in kitchens all over New Orleans—you guessed it—the day after Thanksgiving. In fact, rumor has it New Orleanians tolerate Thanksgiving only in order to get the turkey carcasses to make this gumbo.

....

Serves 8

1 turkey carcass

4 to 5 quarts water

3/4 cup vegetable oil

1/2 cup all-purpose flour

1 pound andouille or other smoked
    sausage, cut into 1/4-inch slices

2 to 3 cups cut-up turkey meat

1 large onion, chopped

1 green bell pepper, chopped

2 stalks celery, chopped

5 cloves garlic, minced

2 cups sliced fresh okra

1 large tomato, chopped

1 (6-ounce) can tomato paste

2 tablespoons Worcestershire sauce

2 teaspoons Creole seasoning
    (page 34)

2 teaspoons Louisiana hot sauce

5 cups cooked white rice

2 green onions, both white and green
    parts, chopped, for garnish

Make a turkey stock by simmering the carcass in the water for about 2 hours. Strain and reserve the stock, skimming off any fat or impurities.

Make a roux in a skillet by stirring 1/2 cup of the oil with the flour over medium-high heat until dark brown (see page 29). Remove from the heat and reserve.

In a separate skillet over medium-high heat, brown the sausage and the turkey meat in the remaining 1/4 cup oil, then add the onion, bell pepper, celery, garlic, okra, and tomato, stirring until a savory paste is formed, about 15 minutes. Add the reserved stock, along with the tomato paste, Worcestershire sauce, Creole seasoning, and hot sauce. Thicken with the roux. Serve over white rice, garnished with green onion.

Crawfish and Andouille Gumbo

New Orleanians love every variation on seafood gumbo, including this one made all over the city whenever crawfish season is at its height. Mother Nature decides when to hold crawfish season—with several mini-seasons turning up some years, thanks to rain in the Atchafalaya Basin or elsewhere. Anytime Mother Nature wants to declare another crawfish season, you won't here any complaints around my house.

Serves 10

2 pounds andouille or other smoked sausage

2 cups plus 3 tablespoons unsalted butter

2 cups all-purpose flour

4 cups diced onion

4 cups diced celery

2 cups dry sherry

4 large bay leaves

2 pounds crawfish tails, peeled

1/4 cup Louisiana hot sauce

5 tablespoons Worcestershire sauce

1 tablespoon ground black pepper

8 quarts seafood or chicken stock (page 30, 31, or 32)

2 tablespoons salt

5 cups cooked white rice

1/4 cup filé powder

Brown the sausage in a large soup pot over medium heat, then remove it from the pan. In a separate skillet, melt 2 cups of the butter and stir in the flour. Cook, stirring, over medium heat to produce a smooth, medium brown roux (see page 29). Remove the roux from the heat, add some of the diced onion and celery to stop the cooking, and set aside.

Add the remaining 3 tablespoons butter and the remaining onion and celery to the soup pot, stirring to scrape the browned bits of sausage from the bottom. Cook over medium heat until the onion is translucent, 5 to 6 minutes. Add the sherry, bay leaves, crawfish tails, hot sauce, Worcestershire sauce, pepper, stock, and salt. Add the roux, a little at a time, stirring to incorporate. Heat to a slow boil, add the reserved andouille, and cook over medium heat for 45 minutes. Remove and discard the bay leaves. Serve in bowls over white rice, sprinkled with filé powder.

Filé Gumbo

Filé powder is actually ground sassafras leaves, a flavorful thickener. Some people love the distinctive taste of filé, others hate it. Local wisdom holds that you should never use both okra and filé powder in the same gumbo. Like too many cooks, too many thickeners can spoil the broth.

Serves 8 to 10

2 pounds andouille or other smoked
    sausage, sliced into discs

3 cups unsalted butter

3 cups all-purpose flour

4 cups diced onion

4 cups chopped celery

2 cups dry sherry

4 large bay leaves, crushed

3 pounds cooked chicken meat, diced

5 tablespoons Louisiana hot sauce

5 tablespoons Worcestershire sauce

1 tablespoon ground black pepper

1 tablespoon cayenne pepper

8 quarts chicken stock (page 32)

2 tablespoons salt

1/4 cup filé powder

4 or 5 cups cooked white rice

Brown the sausage on both sides in a large pan over medium-high heat. Remove the sausage from the pan, leaving the drippings, and set aside.

Make a roux by combining the butter with the flour in the pan, along with the drippings, stirring constantly over medium heat until the mixture is a medium brown, about 10 minutes (see page 29). Add the onion and celery and cook, stirring, just until translucent, about 5 minutes. Add the sherry, bay leaves, chicken, hot sauce, Worcestershire sauce, black pepper, cayenne pepper, stock, salt, filé, and reserved sausage. Cook until the flavors blend, 25 to 30 minutes. Remove and discard the bay leaves. Serve in soup bowls over white rice.

Gumbo Z'herbes

So many things about New Orleans life—starting with Mardi Gras before Ash Wednesday and working from there—stem from the city's Catholic heritage. Since in the old days, just about everybody was Catholic, just about everybody was living by the same church calendar. During Lent, you weren't supposed to eat meat. The result, over time, was this gumbo made without meat or seafood, called gumbo des herbes—or gumbo z'herbes *in the Creole patois.*

Serves 8 to 10

1 bunch collard greens
1 bunch mustard greens
1 bunch turnip greens
1 bunch green onions
1 bunch beet greens
1 bunch carrot greens
1 bunch radish greens
1 small head of cabbage
1 small head Romaine lettuce
1 small head iceberg lettuce
1 bunch chicory
1 cup unsalted butter
1 cup chopped onion
1 cup chopped celery
1 cup chopped green bell pepper
8 cups water
2 teaspoons salt
1/4 teaspoon ground black pepper
1/4 teaspoon cayenne pepper
2 bay leaves
2 whole cloves
6 whole allspice
1/4 teaspoon dried thyme
1/4 teaspoon dried marjoram
4 or 5 cups cooked white rice

Rinse and clean all of the greens, removing any heavy veins. In a large pot over medium heat, melt the butter. Sauté the onion, celery, and bell pepper until opaque, then add all of the greens and sauté until wilted. Add the water, salt, black pepper, cayenne pepper, bay leaves, cloves, allspice, thyme, and marjoram. Bring to a boil, lower the heat, and simmer for $1^{1/2}$ to 2 hours, until tender. Add more water if necessary. Remove and discard the bay leaves and whole spices. Serve in soup bowls over white rice.

Duck Gumbo

South Louisiana men (and no small number of south Louisiana women) love to hunt just about anything that runs, walks, swims, or flies. Duck hunting season is always in the wintertime, when everybody wants a good hot bowl of gumbo anyway. Here's a recipe that certainly started in the duck camps, where hunters like to outcook each other as much as they like to outshoot each other.

....

Serves 8 to 10

1 (3- or-4-pound) duck

4 cups chopped onion

4 cups chopped green bell pepper

4 cups chopped celery

4 bay leaves

8 quarts water

4 cups chicken stock (page 32)

2 cups sliced jumbo mushrooms

1 cup red wine

1/2 pound andouille or other smoked
   sausage, sliced thin

6 tablespoons dark brown roux
   (page 29)

2 tablespoons Worcestershire sauce

3 tablespoons file powder

1 tablespoon ground black pepper

1 tablespoon salt

2 tablespoons Louisiana hot sauce

1/2 cup dry sherry

4 or 5 cups cooked white rice

Skin the duck. Set the skin aside. In a stockpot, place the duck with the innards and neck, 2 cups each of the onion, bell pepper, and celery, the bay leaves, and the water. Bring to a boil over high heat and cook for about 1 1/2 hours. Strain, reserving the liquid, which should be reduced to 4 cups. Discard the vegetables. Remove the meat from the duck, cutting it into 1/2-inch pieces. Remove the meat from the neck and chop up the liver, gizzards, and heart. Set the meat aside.

In a frying pan over medium heat, sauté the duck skin to render the fat. Remove from the heat, and remove and discard the duck skin. In a soup pot, place 1/4 cup of the rendered duck fat and the remaining 2 cups each of the chopped onion, bell pepper, and celery. Sauté the mixture until it is opaque, about 10 minutes. Add the duck stock and chicken stock to the pot. Bring the liquid to a boil. Add the mushrooms, wine, sausage, roux, Worcestershire sauce, filé, pepper, salt, and hot sauce, stirring in the roux very well. Return to a boil, lower the heat, and simmer for about 45 minutes. Add the sherry just before serving. Remove and discard the bay leaves. Serve in soup bowls over white rice.

Oyster Gumbo

During oyster season, which means any month with an "r" in it, which means any month except the summer hotboxes called May, June, July, and August, oysters are a regular, beloved part of New Orleans life. And if we like something in anything, we love it in gumbo.

· ·

Serves 14 to 16

1/2 cup unsalted butter

2 cups chopped green bell pepper

2 cups chopped onion

2 cups chopped celery

6 quarts oyster water (page 23) or clam juice

6 cups sliced fresh okra

3 tablespoons filé powder

3 tablespoons Worcestershire sauce

3 tablespoons Louisiana hot sauce

4 bay leaves

3 tablespoons salt

1 tablespoon coarsely ground black pepper

1 cup chopped fresh parsley

1 cup chopped green onion, both white and green parts

24 to 30 fresh shucked oysters

7 or 8 cups cooked white rice

In an 8-quart soup pot, melt the butter and add the bell pepper, onion, and celery. Sauté until opaque, about 10 minutes. Add the oyster water and okra. Bring to a boil, lower the heat, and simmer for about 30 minutes. Add the filé, Worcestershire sauce, hot sauce, bay leaves, salt, pepper, parsley, and green onion. Continue cooking for another 30 minutes. Add the oysters and cook just until they curl, 5 to 8 minutes. Check and adjust the seasoning. Remove and discard the bay leaves. Serve in soup bowls over white rice.

Catfish Gumbo

For a long time, the catfish was a trash fish extraordinaire—not only an undesirable bottom feeder but a scoundrel that took your bait off the hook to boot. Now that Mississippi (and to some degree, Louisiana) grows farm-raised catfish, the taste is great and the convenience is greater. Give this gumbo a try.

Serves 6 to 8

1/4 cup vegetable oil

1/4 cup all-purpose flour

1 large onion, chopped

1 medium green bell pepper, chopped

3 stalks celery, chopped

4 cloves garlic, minced

4 cups seafood stock (page 30 or 31)

1 (16-ounce) can chopped tomatoes

2 cups chopped okra

1 teaspoon salt

1/2 teaspoon dried thyme

1/2 teaspoon cayenne pepper

1/2 teaspoon dried oregano

1 bay leaf

4 catfish fillets, cut into 1-inch cubes

3 or 4 cups cooked white rice

Make a dark brown roux in a Dutch oven or large, heavy saucepan by stirring the oil and flour together over medium-high heat until a dark brown color is achieved (see page 29). Add the onion, bell pepper, celery, and garlic, stirring until softened, about 10 minutes. Pour in the seafood stock, along with the tomatoes, okra, salt, thyme, cayenne pepper, oregano, and bay leaf. Bring the mixture to a boil, lower the heat, cover, and simmer until the flavors are blended, about 40 minutes. Add the catfish and simmer only 15 minutes more, until the fish flakes easily with a fork. Remove and discard the bay leaf. Serve in soup bowls over white rice.

Mirliton Gumbo

Call them what you will: mirlitons, chayotes, or vegetable pears, these things are good. Here's a gumbo recipe based on one created by veteran Creole chef Austin Leslie for the Mirliton Festival in the city's historic Bywater section some years ago.

Serves 10 to 12

3 medium mirlitons (chayotes)

1 cup unsalted butter

1 onion, finely chopped

1 stalk celery, finely chopped

1 small green bell pepper, finely chopped

6 cloves garlic, finely chopped

2 green onions, both white and green parts, finely chopped

4 sprigs parsley, finely chopped

1/2 cup all-purpose flour

4 bay leaves

1 tablespoon dried thyme

1/2 pound smoked ham, diced

1 pound andouille or other smoked sausage, cut in 1/4-inch slices

6 crabs, cleaned and quartered

1/2 pound medium (31/35) shrimp, peeled and deveined

1 tablespoon Creole seasoning (page 34)

5 or 6 cups cooked white rice

In a large pot of water, boil the mirlitons until they are crisp-tender, 20 to 25 minutes. Drain, reserving the water, and peel, seed, and dice the mirlitons. In another pot, over medium heat, melt the butter and sauté the onion, celery, bell pepper, garlic, green onions, and parsley until the onions are translucent and just golden, about 15 minutes. Stir in the flour and cook, stirring, until brown, about 15 minutes. Add the reserved mirliton stock, bay leaves, and thyme. Heat the liquid for 20 minutes, then stir in the ham, sausage, crabs, and dicedmirlitons. Cook for 30 minutes. Bring to a boil. Add the shrimp and cook just until pink, about 5 minutes. Add the Creole seasoning. Remove and discard the bay leaves. Serve in soup bowls over white rice.

Red Bean Gumbo

Who said you can't put red beans in gumbo? Surely not New Orleans music legend Louis Armstrong, who probably tried putting red beans in everything at one time or another. Red beans and rice is a dish that links New Orleans cuisine to the many economical rice and beans meals of the Caribbean.

Serves 8

1/2 cup vegetable oil

1/2 cup all-purpose flour

1 pound andouille or other smoked sausage, sliced

1 large onion, chopped

1 large green bell pepper, chopped

3 stalks celery, chopped

4 cloves garlic, chopped

1/2 cup chopped fresh parsley

10 cups chicken stock (page 32)

4 cups cooked red kidney beans, or 2 (15-ounce) cans red kidney beans

1 tablespoon Creole seasoning (page 34)

1 tablespoon Worcestershire sauce

1 teaspoon Louisiana hot sauce

4 cups cooked white rice

1/4 cup chopped green onion, both white and green parts, for garnish

Make a dark brown roux in a large saucepan or stew pot by stirring the oil and the flour together over medium-high heat until a dark brown color is achieved (see page 29). Add the sausage, along with the onion, bell pepper, celery, garlic, and parsley, stirring until the vegetables are softened, about 10 minutes. Pour in the chicken stock and add the red beans. Add the Creole seasoning, Worcestershire, and hot sauce, using more if desired. Bring the liquid to a boil, lower the heat, and simmer for 2 hours, until the gumbo is dark and thick. Serve in soup bowls over white rice, garnished with green onion.

Jambalayas

THERE IS NO BETTER PARTY, FESTIVAL, or just plain clean-out-your-fridge food than jambalaya, a rice dish that some say was invented in south Louisiana by the Spanish. Those who argue for a Spanish origin point out that jambalaya has much in common with paella, the Spanish rice dish loaded with meat and seafood. They also claim that the word *jambalaya* is rooted in the Spanish *jamon*, meaning ham, the kind of meat often used to add extra flavor to the rice.

On the other hand, there are those who claim that jambalaya is a French invention, whether in Creole New Orleans or the Cajun countryside. While everyone loves to cite the Spanish *jamon* as though the word seals the deal, the French word for ham is *jambon*—if anything, closer to the business end of jambalaya. Some historians cite the legend of a French Creole who wandered into an inn late at night and asked the cook to whip up whatever he could find. Accord to this tale, the cook's name was Jean, producing the request, "Jean, *belayez.*" This would mean, "Jean, throw something together."

Whether Spanish or French in origin, jambalaya is all about Louisiana now, enjoying its prominence as one of the best-ever ways to make something wonderful out of anything and everything in your refrigerator. As with gumbo, étouffée, and several other important New Orleans dishes, there are thousands of cooks who believe they know the only way to make jambalaya. Chicken, sausage, seafood—some cooks even make steak jambalaya, when they've got some of the expensive stuff lying around.

The great divide in jambalayas is between brown ones and red ones. Brown ones get their color from stock, gravy, or just the browning of the vegetables. Red jambalayas get their color from tomatoes. Like tomato-based shrimp Creole, jambalaya made with tomatoes is sometimes called Creole jambalaya. Take it from an objective observer, both brown and red jambalayas can be terrific.

Chicken and Sausage Jambalaya

Chicken and sausage go together so well with New Orleans' spice profile that they had to be featured in their own jambalaya sooner or later. One taste of this and you'll be glad it was sooner.

....

Serves 10

1/2 cup unsalted butter

3 cups chopped celery

3 cups chopped green bell pepper

3 cups chopped onion

1 pound boneless chicken breast, cut into bite-sized pieces

1 pound andouille or other smoked sausage, thinly sliced

1 tablespoon Creole seasoning (page 34)

1 tablespoon coarsely ground black pepper

3 tablespoons Louisiana hot sauce

3 bay leaves

1 (28-ounce) can crushed tomatoes in their juice

8 cups chicken stock (page 32)

4 cups uncooked long-grain white rice

In a 3-quart saucepan over medium heat, melt the butter and sauté the celery, bell pepper, and onion until the onion is translucent, 8 to 10 minutes. Stir in the chicken and sausage and cook until the chicken is done, 6 to 8 minutes. Add the Creole seasoning, pepper, hot sauce, bay leaves, tomatoes, and chicken stock. Bring to a boil, add the rice, and return to a boil. Cover the pot with a tight-fitting lid, turn off the heat, and let the jambalaya sit until all the liquid is absorbed by the rice, about 20 minutes. Remove and discard the bay leaves. Fluff with a fork and serve in a bowl.

Creole Seafood Jambalaya

If jambalaya really is a descendant of Spanish paella, as some maintain around multicultural New Orleans, this version might be considered the missing link. Paella doesn't usually include crawfish, but I think that's only because the Spaniards of old Valencia didn't know what they were missing.

Serves 10

1/2 cup unsalted butter

3 cups chopped celery

3 cups chopped onion

3 cups chopped green bell pepper

1 pound peeled crawfish tails, with fat

1 pound peeled small (36/45) shrimp

1/2 pint fresh shucked oysters

1 tablespoon Creole seasoning
(page 34)

1 tablespoon coarsely ground black
pepper

1 tablespoon Louisiana hot sauce

1/4 teaspoon dried thyme

3 bay leaves

1 (28-ounce) can crushed plum
tomatoes, with their juice

4 cups oyster water (page 23) or clam
juice

4 cups chicken stock (page 32)

4 cups uncooked long-grain white rice

In a 3-quart saucepan, melt the butter over medium heat and sauté the celery, onion, and bell pepper until the onion is translucent, 8 to 10 minutes. Add the crawfish, shrimp, and oysters, cooking just until the shrimp are pink and the oysters begin to curl at the edges, 5 minutes. Add the Creole seasoning, pepper, hot sauce, thyme, bay leaves, tomatoes, oyster water, and chicken stock. Bring to a boil, stir in the rice, and bring to a second boil. Cover the pot with a tight-fitting lid, turn off the heat, and let sit until the liquid is absorbed by the rice, about 20 minutes. Remove and discard the bay leaves. Fluff with a fork and serve in bowls.

Brown Jambalaya

Here's a strange but delicious jambalaya that takes up with another of New Orleans' beloved rice dishes, dirty rice. Between the chicken livers and the Worcestershire, the dark color will be eye-catching, the flavors bright and exciting.

....

Serves 16

¹/₂ cup unsalted butter

¹/₂ pound andouille or other smoked sausage, thinly sliced

3 cups chopped onion

3 cups chopped celery

3 cups chopped green bell pepper

¹/₂ pound chopped boneless chicken breast

1 pound chicken livers, sautéed and chopped

10 cups chicken stock (page 32)

2 bay leaves

¹/₄ cup Worcestershire sauce

3 tablespoons Louisiana hot sauce

1 teaspoon coarsely ground black pepper

1 teaspoon cayenne pepper

2 teaspoons Creole seasoning (page 34)

4 cups uncooked long-grain white rice

In a 3-quart saucepan, melt the butter over medium heat and sauté the sausage until brown, then sauté the onion, celery, and bell pepper until the onion is translucent, 8 to 10 minutes. Add the chicken breast and livers and stir until the chicken is cooked, about 7 minutes. Add the chicken stock, bay leaves, Worcestershire sauce, hot sauce, black pepper, cayenne pepper, and Creole seasoning. Bring to a boil and cook for about 10 minutes. Stir in the rice, and bring to a second boil. Remove the pot from the heat, cover with a tight-fitting lid, and let sit until all the liquid is absorbed by the rice, 20 to 25 minutes. Remove and discard the bay leaves. Fluff with a fork and serve in bowls.

Oyster Jambalaya

Every year, when fall rolls around, the local fancy turns to oysters—oysters in anything, oysters in everything. Note that this jambalaya is made with cooked rice, so the oysters don't overcook. After all, you've waited a long, hot New Orleans summer for this.

Serves 8

5 dozen fresh oysters

1/2 pound salt pork, cut into small cubes

2 tablespoons vegetable oil

3 medium onions, chopped

2 medium green bell peppers, chopped

2 stalks celery, chopped

3 cloves garlic, chopped

2 large tomatoes, chopped

1 tablespoon Creole seasoning (page 34)

4 cups cooked white rice

1/4 cup chopped green onion, both white and green parts, for garnish

Shuck the oysters, reserving 1 cup oyster water (see page 23). In a deep iron pot, fry the salt pork in the oil over medium-high heat until brown and crisp. Remove the pork and stir in the onions, bell peppers, celery, and garlic, cooking until the vegetables are softened, about 10 minutes. Add the reserved oyster water and tomatoes, cooking until the liquid starts to thicken. Return the fried pork to the pan along with the oysters. Season with Creole seasoning and mix in the cooked rice. Heat through for about 5 minutes and serve in bowls, garnished with green onion.

Boucherie Pork Jambalaya

Just as oyster jambalaya is associated with autumn (even with the hot, steamy autumns we sometimes suffer through in New Orleans), pork jambalaya is associated with the Cajun event known as boucherie in the chilly winter. In a boucherie, in the country, a pig is slaughtered and turned into, well, just about every kind of food a pig can possibly be turned into. Cajuns, it's said, use everything but the squeal. And just about everything can be put into this terrific boucherie jambalaya.

Serves 8

3/4 pound andouille or other smoked sausage, cut into discs

1/4 cup vegetable oil

1 pound lean pork, cut into 1-inch chunks

1 teaspoon Creole seasoning (page 34)

2 medium onions, chopped

1 small green bell pepper, chopped

1 small red bell pepper, chopped

3 stalks celery, chopped

4 green onions, both white and green parts, chopped

4 cloves garlic, minced

2 1/2 cups chicken stock (page 32)

1 1/4 cups uncooked long-grain white rice

In a Dutch oven or large, heavy saucepan, brown the sausage in the oil over medium-high heat, then add the pork chunks, sprinkle with the Creole seasoning, and stir until browned, about 8 minutes. Add the onions, bell peppers, celery, green onions, and garlic, cooking until they are softened, about 10 minutes. Carefully pour the stock into the pot and stir in the rice. Bring the stock to a boil, lower the heat, cover, and simmer until the rice is tender and the liquid is absorbed, about 20 minutes. Fluff with a fork and serve in bowls.

Duck Camp Jambalaya

Another cold-weather favorite! During duck season, there are more duck-hunting widows than football widows in New Orleans. Happily, there's lots of duck jambalaya as well.

Serves 8 to 10

1 medium duck, cut into small serving
   pieces
2 tablespoons Creole seasoning
   (page 34)
3 tablespoons vegetable oil
2 medium onions, chopped
1 medium green bell pepper, chopped
2 stalks celery, chopped
4 cloves garlic, minced
1/4 cup chopped fresh parsley
2 cups uncooked long-grain white rice
4 cups chicken stock (page 32)

Sprinkle the duck pieces with Creole seasoning. Brown them in the oil in a large skillet or saucepan over medium-high heat. Remove the duck and stir in the onions, bell pepper, celery, garlic, and parsley, cooking until the vegetables are softened, about 10 minutes. Return the duck pieces to the pan, add the rice and chicken stock, and bring the liquid to a boil. Lower the heat, cover the pan, and simmer until the rice is cooked and all the liquid is absorbed, 20 to 25 minutes. Serve in large bowls.

Shrimp and Eggplant Jambalaya

Eggplant in New Orleans, though borrowed from the Greeks who borrowed it from the Turks, is always a Sicilian thing. This jambalaya clearly owes as much to places like Messina and Palermo as it does to Golden Meadow or Pointe a la Hache.

....

Serves 8

1 medium eggplant

1 teaspoon vegetable oil

1 medium onion, chopped

1 medium green bell pepper, chopped

2 stalks celery, chopped

1 cup chopped tomatoes

6 cloves garlic, minced

2 cups chicken stock (page 32)

1 cup uncooked long-grain white rice

1 pound medium (31/35) shrimp,
   peeled and deveined

Peel and dice the eggplant, then fry it in the oil in a large saucepan over medium-high heat until golden brown. Add the onion, bell pepper, celery, tomatoes, and garlic. Cook, stirring, until the vegetables are softened, 8 to 10 minutes. Pour in the chicken stock and rice. Bring to a boil, lower the heat, cover, and simmer for 10 minutes. Add the shrimp and contine to simmer until the rice is cooked and all the liquid is absorbed, another 10 minutes. Serve in bowls.

New Year's Jambalaya

What makes for a happy and prosperous new year? Black-eyed peas, of course. If you need a fix of jambalaya and a fix of good luck as the old year counts down to midnight, do we ever have the recipe for you.

....

Serves 6 to 8

1½ pounds andouille or other smoked
    sausage
¼ cup vegetable oil
1 large onion, chopped
1 medium green bell pepper, chopped
3 stalks celery, chopped
2 cloves garlic, minced
2 tablespoons Creole seasoning
    (page 34)
2 cups chicken stock (page 32)
2 tablespoons minced pimiento
1 cup uncooked long-grain white rice
1½ cups cooked black-eyed peas
¼ cup chopped green onion, both
    white and green parts, for garnish

Brown the sausage in the oil in a large saucepan over medium-high heat. Add the onion, bell pepper, celery, garlic, and Creole seasoning. Cook, stirring, until the vegetables are softened, about 10 minutes. Add the stock, pimiento, rice, and black-eyed peas, bringing the mixture to a boil. Lower the heat, cover the pot, and cook until the rice is tender and all the liquid is absorbed, 20 to 25 minutes. Serve in bowls, garnished with green onion.

Étouffées and Court-Bouillons

HAPPILY, IN A CHAPTER SHOWCASING ÉTOUFFÉES and court-bouillons, along with a New Orleans spin on bouillabaisse, the dishes are easier to make than they are to spell. As usual in New Orleans, all three words are found in the language and cuisine of France—but not one of these dishes is found in the form it takes here.

Étouffée means simply "smothered," a culinary reference to any dish slow-cooked in a liquid that pretty much forms a gravy as it cooks. Traditionally, étouffées are cooked in a covered pot, to keep the moisture from evaporating during the extended cooking period, which traditionally was associated with and even required by lesser cuts of meat. Ironically, the benchmark étouffée for the entire state of Louisiana is crawfish, followed in popularity by shrimp and chicken. Crawfish are tender and cook quickly, so there's no real excuse for "smothering" them, other than the fact that they taste incredible cooked that way. Finally, while étouffée now stands as a classic claimed by both Creoles and Cajuns, history and style point toward origins among the Cajuns in the countryside.

If étouffées have become more commonplace in recent years, with the incorporation of long-foreign Cajun dishes into New Orleans cooking, the opposite has occurred with court-bouillon. French for "short broth," a court-bouillon is the essence of Creole, a kind of quick-poached fish dish given color and taste by tomatoes. Never to be confused with any bland broth of the same name in France, the classic is redfish court-bouillon—an unusually subtle and elegant presentation of a delicate fish now usually subjected to heavy-handed blackening. During the 1980s, when the blackening craze went global and a federal moratorium had to be issued to save the redfish, New Orleans cooks started trying other fish in their court-bouillons. As expected, considering the freshness and flavor of local fish, the results were always impressive.

Finally, bouillabaisse is not from New Orleans. But it does hail from Marseilles, the ancient French port city that gave New Orleans some of its earliest restaurateurs—including Antoine Alciatore, who founded Antoine's in 1840. For all the "requirements" placed upon it by chefs in and around Marseilles, bouillabaisse is actually just a solid and sumptuous seafood stew. In recent years, New Orleans chefs have excelled at taking the basics from the old French port, substituting a wide variety of Louisiana seafood and giving this unforgettable stew a sizzling Creole-Cajun spin.

Crawfish Étouffée

Crawfish étouffée is one of the essential dishes of Cajun cooking, one that came into the city from the country and found a lot of happy mouths to feed. No restaurant in south Louisiana can turn out enough of this stuff when the crawfish are running big, fat, and juicy along the bayous of the Atchafalaya Basin.

Serves 6

1/4 cup unsalted butter

1 cup chopped onion

1 cup chopped celery

1 cup chopped green bell pepper

1 pound crawfish tail meat, peeled

2 bay leaves

1 tablespoon grated lemon zest

1/4 cup sherry

1/2 tablespoon ground black pepper

1/2 tablespoon Creole seasoning
   (page 34)

3 tablespoons Louisiana hot sauce

1 teaspoon cayenne pepper

1/2 tablespoon chile powder

2 teaspoons salt

3 cups chicken stock (page 32)

1 cup dark brown roux (page 29)

3 cups cooked white rice

In a large stockpot, melt the butter over medium-high heat. Sauté the onion, celery, and bell pepper until the onion is translucent, 7 to 10 minutes. Add the crawfish, bay leaves, and lemon zest and cook for 2 minutes. Add the sherry, black pepper, Creole seasoning, hot sauce, cayenne pepper, chile powder, and salt. Sauté for 1 minute. Add the stock and bring to a boil. Whisk in the roux until the desired consistency is reached. Cover pot and simmer for 20 to 30 minutes. Remove and discard the bay leaves. Serve in bowls over white rice.

Shrimp Étouffée

In terms of popularity across south Louisiana, shrimp étouffée comes in a close second to crawfish, at least partly because crawfish is a fickle crop subject to rains and other conditions in the Atchafalaya Basin. Shrimp, on the other hand, usually have several seasons, which is good news indeed.

....

Serves 8

1/2 cup unsalted butter

1/4 cup all-purpose flour

4 medium onions, chopped

2 medium green bell peppers, chopped

2 stalks celery, chopped

2 cloves garlic, minced

1 teaspoon tomato paste

2 pounds medium (31/35) shrimp,
    peeled and deveined

1 cup shrimp stock (page 30)

1 tablespoon Creole seasoning
    (page 34)

3/4 cup chopped green onion, both
    white and green parts

2 tablespoons chopped fresh parsley

4 cups cooked white rice

Melt the butter over medium heat in a large skillet and stir in the flour. Cook, stirring, to make a light brown roux (see page 29). Add the onions, bell peppers, celery, and garlic and cook, stirring, until the vegetables are softened, about 10 minutes. Blend in the tomato paste. Add the shrimp and cook just until they turn pink, about 5 minutes. Add the stock and stir until the sauce starts to thicken, then add the Creole seasoning, green onion, and parsley. Cover the pot and simmer for 15 minutes. Serve in bowls over white rice.

Drumfish Étouffée

Think you've never heard of drumfish? You have if you've ever eaten a blackened redfish. Redfish is officially a red drum, and kissing kin to black drum—which filled in quite nicely when the federal government was saving our overfished big reds. There are actually several types of drumfish. All are good for blackening, for making court-bouillon, and for whipping up this delicious étouffée.

Serves 8 to 10

5 pounds drumfish fillets, cut into large pieces

1 teaspoon salt

1 teaspoon ground black pepper

1/4 teaspoon cayenne pepper

3 tablespoons vegetable oil

1 medium onion, chopped

1 medium green bell pepper, chopped

2 stalks celery, chopped

4 cloves garlic, minced

1 bunch fresh parsley, chopped

1 bay leaf

2 tablespoons all-purpose flour

1 1/2 cups tomato sauce

1/4 teaspoon dried thyme

2 slices lemon

1/2 cup water

4 or 5 cups cooked white rice

4 green onions, both white and green parts, chopped, for garnish

Season the fish pieces with the salt, black pepper, and cayenne pepper. Pour the oil into an unheated pot, arrange the fish on the bottom, and place about half the chopped onion, bell pepper, celery, garlic, and parsley, and the bay leaf over the fish. Sprinkle half the flour and tomato sauce over the vegetables, then top with the remaining vegetables, flour, and tomato sauce. Add the thyme, lemon, and water. Place the pot over a low flame and cook until the fish is tender, about 1 hour, shaking the pot occasionally to keep the fish from sticking. Do not break up the fish. Remove and discard the bay leaf and lemon rinds. Serve in bowls over white rice and garnish with green onion.

Chicken Étouffée

In the Cajun country of southwest Louisiana, not everybody lives on the water. Even a famous Cajun like Paul Prudhomme spent more time working on his family's inland farm than fishing from a dock on some bayou. So just about all Cajun recipes have land versions and water versions. This is a land version of étouffée.

Serves 8

1/2 cup unsalted butter

3/4 cup all-purpose flour

6 chicken breast halves, cut into bite-sized pieces

2 medium onions, chopped

2 medium green bell peppers, chopped

2 stalks celery, chopped

4 green onions, both white and green parts, chopped

4 cloves garlic, minced

2 teaspoons dried thyme

1 teaspoon dried basil

2 teaspoons salt

2 teaspoons ground black pepper

1 teaspoon cayenne pepper

2 teaspoons chile powder

1 teaspoon ground cloves

6 cups chicken stock (page 32)

4 cups cooked white rice

Melt the butter in a large saucepan over medium heat. Stir in the flour and make a roux by cooking and stirring until a caramel color is achieved (see page 29). Add the chicken and stir until browned, about 5 minutes. Then add the onions, bell peppers, celery, green onions, and garlic, cooking until the vegetables are softened, about 8 minutes. Add the thyme, basil, salt, black pepper, cayenne pepper, chile powder, and cloves, simmering for about3 minutes to release their flavors. Slowly pour in the chicken stock and bring to a boil. Reduce the heat and simmer for 30 minutes. Serve in bowls over white rice.

Duck and Sausage Étouffée

Even when you wander off from duck and sausage gumbo, duck and sausage remain a dizzyingly tasty combination. Here, the two join forces to produce a hearty country-style étouffée, one at least a day's wagon ride from the delicate variations dished up in the big city of New Orleans.

Serves 8 to 10

1/2 cup unsalted butter

6 boneless duck breasts, cut into bite-sized pieces

1 tablespoon Creole seasoning (page 34)

1 pound andouille or other smoked sausage, cut into small cubes

1 medium onion, chopped

1 medium green bell pepper, chopped

4 cloves garlic, minced

1 (16-ounce) can diced tomatoes

1 teaspoon dried thyme

1 teaspoon dried oregano

1/4 cup all-purpose flour

5 cups duck or chicken stock (page 33 or 32)

4 or 5 cups cooked white rice

1/2 cup chopped green onion, both white and green parts, for garnish

Melt the butter in a large, heavy saucepan over medium-high heat. Sprinkle the duck with the Creole seasoning, then brown it in the butter with the sausage. Add the onion, bell pepper, garlic, tomatoes, thyme, and oregano and cook, stirring, until the vegetables are softened, about 10 minutes. Stir in the flour and cook, stirring, until any lumps are gone and a medium brown roux is formed (see page 29). Carefully pour in the stock, lower the heat, and simmer for about 10 minutes. Serve in bowls over white rice, garnished with green onion.

Redfish Court-Bouillon

When New Orleanians think of court-bouillon (and we do, more often than might be healthy), we think of redfish court-bouillon. With its blend of French technique and Spanish tomatoes, this court-bouillon is like shrimp Creole that struck it rich. Be careful to not overcook the fish.

....

Serves 6

1/4 cup vegetable oil

1/4 cup all-purpose flour

1 medium onion, chopped

1 medium green bell pepper, chopped

2 stalks celery, chopped

2 cloves garlic, minced

3 large tomatoes, chopped

1 tablespoon minced fresh parsley

2 bay leaves

1/2 teaspoon dried thyme

1/2 teaspoon dried basil

2 teaspoons Creole seasoning
   (page 34)

3 tablespoons freshly squeezed lemon
   juice

1/2 cup dry red wine

3 cups water

1 medium redfish (4 to 5 pounds),
   cleaned and cut into 2-inch slices

8 slices lemon

Make a medium brown roux by combining the oil with the flour in a large soup pot or kettle, stirring constantly over medium heat until it is the color of peanut butter (see page 29). Add the onion, bell pepper, celery, and garlic and cook, stirring, until the vegetables are softened, about 10 minutes. Add the tomatoes, parsley, bay leaves, thyme, basil, Creole seasoning, lemon juice, and wine. Slowly add the water. Bring to a boil, lower the heat, and simmer, uncovered, for about 30 minutes. Add the redfish and lemon slices and simmer for 10 minutes, just until the fish flakes easily with a fork. Remove and discard the bay leaves and lemon rinds. Serve in bowls.

Catfish Court-Bouillon

Everything nice we've said about redfish court-bouillon applies here too. This court-bouillon has gotten cheaper and easier to make with the proliferation of clean-tasting farm-raised catfish in neighboring Mississippi and now in Louisiana. It weighs in without the wine but with a little extra heat. Hardly necessary, but a good touch.

Serves 8

Vegetable oil

1 medium onion, chopped

1 medium green bell pepper, chopped

2 stalks celery, chopped

4 cloves garlic, minced

1 (10-ounce) can Ro-Tel tomatoes or 3 medium tomatoes, chopped

2 (15-ounce) cans tomato sauce

2 tablespoons dark brown roux (page 29)

2 cups seafood stock (page 30 or 31) or water

3 pounds catfish fillets

1 or 2 teaspoons Creole seasoning (page 34)

4 cups cooked white rice

$1/2$ cup chopped fresh parsley, for garnish

$3/4$ cup chopped green onion, both white and green parts, for garnish

In a large soup pot, heat just enough oil to coat the bottom. Stir in the onion, bell pepper, celery, and garlic and cook until softened, about 10 minutes. Add the tomatoes and tomato sauce, cooking until a thickened paste starts to form. Stir in the roux and the stock, making sure the roux is dissolved. Lower the heat and simmer for $1^1/2$ hours. Add the catfish about 20 minutes before serving, shaking the pot rather than stirring to keep the fillets intact. Add the Creole seasoning. Serve in bowls over cooked white rice, garnished with parsley and green onion.

Crescent City Bouillabaisse

We in New Orleans can never leave well enough alone. We can picture some early Creole chef, listening to his counterpart from Marseilles pontificate on just which fish and just how much he needs to use to produce an authentic bouillabaisse. Eventually, in New Orleans, the teacher always went home to France—and we learned to really make bouillabaisse. We made it with our seafood. And we made it our way.

Serves 10

1 pint fresh oysters
1/2 cup unsalted butter
1/2 cup all-purpose flour
1 large onion, chopped
1 medium green bell pepper, chopped
2 stalks celery, chopped
4 cloves garlic, minced
1 large tomato, chopped
2 bay leaves
2 tablespoons chopped fresh parsley
1/2 cup dry white wine
8 cups cold water
1 tablespoon Creole seasoning (page 34)
1/4 teaspoon saffron
2 tablespoons lemon juice
2 pounds redfish fillets
1 pound speckled trout fillets
1 cup lump crabmeat
1 cup peeled crawfish tails, fat reserved

1 1/2 pounds medium (31/35) shrimp, peeled and deveined
Sliced French bread

Shuck the oysters, reserving the oyster water (see page 23). Melt the butter in an 8-quart soup pot over medium heat. Stir in the flour and make a medium brown roux by cooking and stirring until the mixture is the color of peanut butter (see page 29). Add the onion, bell pepper, celery, and garlic and cook, stirring, until the vegetables are softened, about 10 minutes. Add the tomato, bay leaves, parsley, reserved oyster water, wine, water, Creole seasoning, saffron, and lemon juice. Bring the liquid to a boil, then lower the heat and simmer for 10 minutes. Carefully add the fish fillets and simmer until the fish flakes easily with a fork, about 10 minutes. Then add the oysters, crabmeat, crawfish tails with their fat, and shrimp. Simmer for just 5 minutes, then remove from the heat and let stand for 5 minutes more. Remove and discard the bay leaves. Place a slice of French bread in each bowl, and gently spoon the bouillabaisse over the top.

Soups

nEW ORLEANS IS A GREAT SOUP TOWN, for all the right reasons. And if you love
soup as much as we do here, there aren't any wrong reasons! For starters, all
three of the major cultures that had the first go at forming New Orleans made
some fine soups. The French, of course, were famous for theirs, particularly the
southern French who did the most populating around here, the people of bouillabaisse, bourride, and beyond. The Spanish (our second overlords) were no soup
slouches either, giving the world caldo from the far northwest in Galicia and
chilled gazpacho from the eastern coast. Finally, Africa had a profound (if underrecognized) soup tradition, turning out stews and broths made of everything from
sweet potatoes to peanuts.

Soup is one of the simplest and most direct presentations of just about any
food. Sure, tricks can be added to any recipe, especially if the one doing the
adding is a chef. But even underneath the tricks, the notion of soup is simplicity
verging on the primal. You take whatever you have, put it in a big pot, and boil it
in water, probably for a very long time. That heat spread over that time lets all the

ingredients cease to be themselves and become part of something bigger, almost certainly something better.

In New Orleans, soups are made with fish, shrimp, crawfish, and crabmeat, not to mention chicken, beef, beans, and vegetables. Some soups are broth-based and mostly natural, taking their flavor from the mingling of broth and seasonings. Other soups (usually the ones you find in restaurants) are cream based, starting with broth more often than not but enriched with enough heavy cream to be a delicious menace to any diet.

And then there are the soups we call bisques. These are thicker and richer than "normal" soups, showing up either as thick, lush, puréed pleasures or as the stand-alone classic, crawfish bisque. Far from being one purée, this unique bisque is distinguished by the crawfish heads stuffed with a mixture of tail meat and bread crumbs that crown the luscious liquid. It takes a lot of work to make south Louisiana crawfish bisque. So by the most real equation I know, it takes (and gives) a lot of love.

Turtle Soup

The tradition of eating turtle began in the often-impoverished south Louisiana countryside. Even today, at ramshackle country grocery stores, you'll see "Turtal Meet" among the items scrawled on the blackboard at the side of the dusty highway. Turtle was enjoyed in New Orleans as well, but in a more refined manner. Turtle soup is an important restaurant dish in the French Quarter, where all night every night waiters give the final, theatrical splash of sherry to one of the city's true classics.

Serves 12

3 pounds turtle meat, diced

1 cup vegetable oil

2 cups medium brown roux (page 29)

2 cups finely chopped onion

1/2 cup chopped green onion, both white and green parts

1 cup finely chopped green bell pepper

1/2 cup finely chopped celery

4 cloves garlic, chopped

1/2 cup finely chopped fresh parsley

4 quarts chicken stock (page 32)

2 cups tomato purée

2 lemons, sliced

4 bay leaves

2 or 3 tablespoons Creole seasoning (page 34)

1/2 teaspoon ground allspice

1 teaspoon ground cloves

8 hard-boiled eggs, chopped

1 cup dry sherry

In a large skillet, heat the oil over medium heat and sauté the turtle meat until brown; set aside. Heat the roux slowly in a large stockpot over medium heat, then stir in the onion, green onion, bell pepper, celery, garlic, and parsley. Stir for 5 minutes. Add the stock, tomato purée, lemon slices, bay leaves, Creole seasoning, allspice, and cloves. Simmer for 1 hour. Add the turtle meat and chopped eggs and simmer for an additional 20 minutes. Remove and discard the bay leaves and lemon rinds. Serve in soup bowls with a splash of sherry as desired.

Crawfish Bisque

Here is one of the classics of Cajun cuisine, a dish light years removed from the smooth, refined bisques served in France. The central pleasure here comes from the stuffed crawfish heads, which are fried in a light batter beforehand.

....

Serves 6

STUFFED CRAWFISH HEADS

1 cup vegetable oil

2 medium onions, chopped

2 green onions, both white and green parts, chopped

1 clove garlic, chopped

2 cups crawfish tails, cut into small pieces

Salt and ground black pepper

Creole seasoning (page 34)

1/4 cup chopped fresh parsley

3 eggs, well beaten

2 cups bread crumbs

30 crawfish heads, eyes and antennae removed

Oil for deep-frying

1 cup milk

To prepare the stuffed heads, heat the oil in a heavy-bottomed pan over medium heat and simmer the onions, green onions, and garlic until tender. Add the chopped crawfish tails and season with salt, pepper, and Creole seasoning. Cook over low heat for 4 minutes, then add the parsley, 2 of the beaten eggs, and the bread crumbs. Mix well. Let the mixture cool and stuff it into the cleaned crawfish heads.

Heat vegetable oil in a deep-fat fryer to 375°F. Prepare a batter with the remaining egg and the milk. Dip the stuffed heads into this batter, then deep-fry for 3 to 5 minutes.

BISQUE

1/2 cup vegetable oil

1/2 cup all-purpose flour

3 large onions, diced

1 clove garlic, minced

2 stalks celery, chopped

1/2 green bell pepper, chopped

8 cups water

Salt and ground black pepper

Creole seasoning (page 34)

1 pinch sugar

1/2 cup crawfish fat (from shells during peeling)

2 pounds crawfish tails, peeled

3 green onions, both white and green parts, chopped

3 cups cooked white rice

1/2 cup chopped fresh parsley, for garnish

To prepare the bisque, make a roux in a heavy-bottomed pan by heating the oil over medium heat and stirring in the flour. Stir constantly until the mixture is golden brown (see page 29). Add the onions, garlic, celery, and bell pepper, stirring to keep the vegetables from burning. Add 6 cups of the water. Season with salt, pepper, Creole seasoning, and sugar. Bring the mixture to a simmer.

In a separate saucepan, combine the remaining 2 cups water with the crawfish fat, stirring over medium heat until it comes to a boil. Add this to the bisque and simmer for 1 hour. Add the peeled whole crawfish tails, green onion, and parsley, and simmer for an additional 30 minutes. Serve in large soup bowls over white rice, garnished with parsley. Set 5 deep-fried stuffed crawfish heads atop each serving of bisque.

Oysters Rockefeller Soup

Oysters Rockefeller, still alleged to be a secret recipe but imitated all over town, was created at Antoine's in the French Quarter and named because it struck the proprietor as being as "rich as Rockefeller." With the cream, it is just that. This creamy soup puts a new spin on the flavor profile of the famed baked oyster dish.

Serves 12

1/2 cup unsalted butter

3 cups diced onion

2 cups diced celery

1/2 cup Pernod

8 cups oyster water (see page 23)
   or clam juice

1 tablespoon Creole seasoning
   (page 34)

3/4 cup all-purpose flour

2 pounds fresh spinach, finely chopped

2 cups heavy cream

3 pints fresh shucked oysters, coarsely
   chopped

2 tablespoons finely chopped green
   onion, both white and green parts,
   for garnish

In a large stockpot, melt 1/4 cup of the butter over high heat and sauté the onion and celery until softened, about 5 minutes. Deglaze the pot by stirring in the Pernod, then add the oyster water and bring to a simmer. Cook for about 12 minutes. Add the Creole seasoning.

Meanwhile, in a small skillet or sauté pan, make a blond roux by combining the remaining 1/4 cup butter with the flour and stirring over medium heat until it just begins to color. Add the roux to the liquid in the stockpot, stirring until it is incorporated. In quick succession, stir in the spinach, cooking only until wilted, followed by the cream and the oysters. Simmer until the oysters start to curl at the edges, about 2 minutes. Serve in soup bowls, garnished with green onion.

Mustard Green Soup

This is New Orleans soul food, a soup that takes the greens enjoyed by the poorest of the poor and turns them into a hearty, soul-satisfying chicken soup.

Serves 6

¹/₄ cup all-purpose flour

¹/₄ cup vegetable oil

1 medium onion, chopped

1 green bell pepper, finely chopped

1 small chicken, cut into small serving pieces

1 medium potato, diced

1 (16-ounce) can white beans

3 bunches mustard or turnip greens, stems removed

6 cups chicken stock (page 32)

1 ham hock

Salt and ground black pepper

Make a roux by stirring the flour and oil together in a large pot and cooking over medium heat until medium brown (see page 29). Add the onion, bell pepper, chicken, and potato. Brown for about 5 minutes, then add the white beans, greens, and stock. Cook until the chicken is tender, about 25 minutes. Remove the chicken pieces, cut the meat from the bones, and return the meat to the soup. Discard the bones. Season to taste with salt and pepper. Serve in soup bowls.

Fish Head Soup

While we're talking soul food, you really should try this soup made with the fish heads left after the fillets have been removed for more refined use. It's a bit like redfish court-bouillon for people who can't afford the redfish. The heads make an amazingly flavorful broth, with an abundance of good meat that will surprise the people who just walked off with the fillets.

Serves 12

12 medium fish heads

1/4 cup olive oil

3 cloves garlic

1 large onion, chopped

1 small green bell pepper, chopped

1 cup red wine

1 (6-ounce) can tomato paste

1 (16-ounce) can whole tomatoes

1 tablespoon minced fresh parsley

1 teaspoon Italian seasoning

Place the fish heads in a large pot, cover with water, and bring to a boil. Lower the heat and simmer for 1 hour. Strain the stock. When the fish heads are cool enough, pick out the meat. Reserve the meat and about 2 cups of the stock. Heat the olive oil in a large soup pot over medium heat and sauté the garlic, onion, and bell pepper until softened, about 7 minutes. Add the wine, tomato paste, and whole tomatoes. Bring just to a simmer. Add the parsley, Italian seasoning, and stock. Add the meat from the fish heads and simmer for about 30 minutes. Serve in soup bowls.

New Orleans Minestrone

Soups like classic Italian minestrone (which means "big soup," since minestra just means "soup" in Italian) made the crossing to New Orleans with boatload after boatload of hungry Sicilians. It was probably one of the dishes they wanted to make as soon as they found a kitchen in their new home, adapting it to the ingredients they found here.

Serves 6

1 or 2 pounds andouille or other smoked sausage, sliced

6 cups beef stock (page 32)

1 cup chopped onion

1/2 cup dry red wine

1 (1-pound) can tomatoes, with their juice

2 cups thinly sliced carrot

1 cup thinly sliced celery

1 cup ketchup

1 tablespoon Creole seasoning (page 34)

2 cloves garlic, minced

2 cups sliced zucchini

8 ounces pasta of your choice

1 medium green bell pepper, diced

1/4 cup chopped fresh parsley

Salt and ground black pepper

Grated Parmesan cheese

Brown the sausage in a skillet, drain, and set it aside. In a large soup pot over medium heat, bring the beef stock to a simmer. Add the sausage, onion, red wine, tomatoes, carrot, celery, ketchup, Creole seasoning, and garlic. Bring to a boil, and lower the heat to a simmer. Simmer for 30 minutes. Add the zucchini, pasta, bell pepper, and parsley. Cover and continue to simmer until the pasta and zucchini are tender, about 15 minutes. Season with salt and pepper. Serve in soup bowls, sprinkled with Parmesan cheese.

Louisiana Yam Soup

Louisiana yams, which are sold as just about everything except what they really are (sweet potatoes), go a long way toward making this colorful, "Out of Africa" soup a bowlful you'll never forget. The crumbled bacon adds just the right crunch at the last minute.

....

Serves 6 to 8

3 cups mashed cooked Louisiana yams

3 tablespoons unsalted butter, at room temperature

1 tablespoon sugar

3 slices bacon

1/2 cup finely chopped onion

2 cups chicken stock (page 32), more if needed

1 cup half-and-half

1/2 teaspoon salt

1/2 teaspoon ground black pepper

1 teaspoon ground nutmeg

In a large bowl, mash the yams with the butter and sugar. In a large saucepan, cook the bacon over medium-high heat just until crisp. Remove from the pan and sauté the onion in the bacon drippings. Crumble the bacon. Add to the onion, along with the chicken stock, half-and-half, salt, pepper, and nutmeg. Add the mashed yams and purée in a blender or food processor. Add more stock if the soup is too thick. Serve in soup bowls.

Alligator Soup

This soup made many friends some years ago, when the green turtle used in New Orleans turtle soup was placed on the government's endangered list. Never ones to put on airs, the Guste family of Antoine's headed out to their swampy hideaway on the north shore of Lake Pontchartrain and started trapping 'gators to make the soup. For quite a long time, until the turtles got their reproductive act together, diners enjoyed swamp alligator in one of the fanciest restaurants in North America.

....

Serves 6 to 8

STOCK

2 pounds cleaned alligator meat

2 stalks celery, coarsely chopped

1 head garlic, peeled and coarsely
  chopped

1 onion, coarsely chopped

Salt

8 cups water

SOUP

1/2 cup all-purpose flour

1/2 cup vegetable oil

3/4 cup chopped onion

3/4 cup chopped leek, white part only

1 cup chopped tomatoes

1 teaspoon Creole seasoning (page 34)

Sherry

2 hard-boiled eggs, chopped, for
  garnish

To prepare the stock, in a large soup pot, combine the alligator with the celery, garlic, and onion. Season with salt; add the water and cook over medium heat for about 30 minutes. Skim if necessary. Strain the stock and keep warm over low heat. Chop the alligator meat into bite-sized pieces; discard the vegetables.

To prepare the soup, in a large skillet over medium heat, stir together the flour and oil and make a roux by cooking and stirring until the mixture is brown (see page 29). Stir in the onion, leeks, and tomatoes, simmering until the onion is just softened. Add the roux mixture and the alligator meat back to the stock. Add the Creole seasoning. Serve in soup bowls, adding a splash of sherry and garnishing the soup with chopped egg.

Cucuzza Soup

Spelled with a "c" but usually pronounced with something resembling a "g," this long green squash is adored by the Sicilians of New Orleans. In fact, traditionally, lots of Sicilians grew cucuzzas in their backyard gardens. If you don't grow cucuzza and can't find anything by that name in your supermarket, most other squashes will work equally well. Winter squashes like acorn, butternut, and hubbard are better than the summer varieties like crookneck, pattypan, and zucchini, because they'll keep their firmness longer. But in the spirit of those Sicilians, adjust to what you can find.

Serves 8

1 medium cucuzza squash or 6 medium zucchini, peeled and cut into bite-sized pieces

2 medium onions, peeled and chopped

2 tablespoons olive oil

1 cup chicken stock (page 32), more if necessary

1 teaspoon Creole seasoning (page 34)

1 teaspoon Louisiana hot sauce

1/4 cup chopped green onion, both white and green parts, for garnish

Boil the cucuzza pieces and onions in a large pot of salted water until they are soft, 25 to 30 minutes. Drain the vegetables and transfer to a mixing bowl. Add the olive oil, chicken stock, Creole seasoning, and hot sauce, then purée the mixture in a blender, adding more stock if it's too thick. Serve in soup bowls, garnished with green onion.

Mirliton Soup

Mirlitons are another vegetable that grows easily and well in most New Orleans backyard gardens. In fact, they grow by other names (chayote, vegetable pear) in so many other parts of the world that there's a virtual global network of mirliton lovers who don't even know one another. Make this soup—and you'll surely make some new friends.

Serves 8

4 medium mirlitons (chayotes), peeled, seeded, and diced

3 tablespoons unsalted butter

1/4 cup vegetable oil

1/4 cup all-purpose flour

6 cups chicken stock (page 32), heated

2 teaspoons ground ginger

Salt and ground white pepper

Toasted French bread croutons, for garnish

Boil the diced mirlitons in water until very tender, about 25 minutes, then mash them with the butter. Make a light brown roux by stirring the oil with the flour in a large pot over medium heat for about 10 minutes (see page 29), then incorporate the chicken stock and mashed mirlitons. Simmer for about 5 minutes. Strain the soup by pressing the liquid through a sieve. Add the ginger and season to taste with salt and white pepper. Serve in soup bowls, garnished with croutons.

Maque Choux Soup

The Cajun smothered corn dish known as maque choux (see page 122) is a wonderful soup waiting to happen. You can use frozen or canned corn, in that order of preference, but using fresh is always better.

....

Serves 6

¹/₃ cup unsalted butter

1 medium onion, finely chopped

1 medium green bell pepper, finely chopped

3 cups fresh corn kernels (from about 5 ears corn)

1 large tomato, chopped

4 cups half-and-half

1 egg, beaten

2 teaspoons Creole seasoning (page 34)

Melt the butter in a large soup pot over medium-high heat and sauté the onion, bell pepper, and corn kernels until they begin to soften, about 10 minutes. Add the tomato, half-and-half, egg, and Creole seasoning. Lower the heat and simmer for about 25 minutes. Serve in soup bowls.

Creole Pepperpot

This soup is a reminder that some have called New Orleans the northernmost Caribbean Island. Pepperpot is the great catchall, use-all soup of islanders from the Bahamas all the way down to South America, taking on the distinct flavors of each island's immigration mix. Here's a solid, well-seasoned version that takes on ours.

Serves 6 to 8

2 pounds collard greens

1/2 pound fresh spinach

1/2 pound salt pork, cut into thin strips

1/2 pound lean pork, cubed

2 medium onions, sliced

2 cups chopped fresh okra

2 jalapeño peppers, seeded and sliced

1 teaspoon dried thyme

1 teaspoon ground cumin

1 or 2 teaspoons Creole seasoning (page 34)

6 cups chicken stock (page 32)

1/4 pound medium (31/35) shrimp, peeled and deveined

Remove all stems from the collard greens and spinach, and wash the leaves thoroughly. In a soup pot, sauté the salt pork over medium heat for 10 minutes, rendering the fat. Add the pork cubes and onions, stirring until the onion is softened, 8 to 10 minutes. Add the collard greens, okra, jalapeños, thyme, cumin, Creole seasoning, and stock. Bring to a boil, then lower the heat, cover, and simmer for 1 1/2 hours. Add the spinach and simmer for another 30 minutes. About 5 minutes before serving, add the shrimp and cook just until they turn pink. Remove the salt pork. Serve in soup bowls.

Pigeon Pea Soup with Dumplings

The dumplings are the distinctive element here, one surely added by generations of Creole cooks remembering a life in the islands and longing to stretch "poor folks'" food for just one more meal. As for the peas or beans, feel free to use any kind you like, from navy beans to baby limas. The cooking time may change a little, but not the fabulous final result.

Serves 8

SOUP

2 cups dried pigeon peas

8 cups water

1 smoked ham hock

2 medium onions, chopped

1 medium green bell pepper, chopped

2 carrots, peeled and chopped

2 stalks celery, chopped

3 cloves garlic, chopped

1 bay leaf

1/2 teaspoon dried rosemary

1 or 2 teaspoons Creole seasoning (page 34)

1/2 pound andouille or other smoked sausage, sliced and browned

1/4 cup chopped green onion, both white and green parts, for garnish

To prepare the soup, wash the peas to remove any grit. Place in a bowl and add enough water to cover. Soak them overnight. Drain the peas and discard the water.

Pour the water into a stockpot and add the ham hock, onions, bell pepper, carrots, celery, garlic, bay leaf, rosemary, and Creole seasoning. Bring the liquid to a boil, lower the heat, and simmer for 45 minutes. Strain the broth, reserving the ham hock and discarding the vegetables. Skim any fat from the broth. Return the broth and the ham hock to the pot, along with the soaked peas. Simmer until the peas are tender, about 2 hours.

DUMPLINGS

1 cup all-purpose flour

¼ cup cornmeal

1 teaspoon sugar

1 teaspoon salt

½ teaspoon ground black pepper

2 tablespoons unsalted butter

⅓ cup water

Meanwhile, prepare the dumplings. Bring a pot of water to a slow boil. Sift together the flour, cornmeal, sugar, salt, and pepper. Using your fingertips, rub in the butter until the dough is crumbly. Add just enough water to form a stiff dough. Form into 1- to 2-inch oblong dumplings. Drop the dumplings into the lightly boiling water and cook until done, about 15 minutes. You should have about 20 dumplings.

When the peas are cooked, remove about half of them with a slotted spoon and purée them, either in a food processor or using a fork to mash them in a bowl. Return the purée to the soup. Add the dumplings and browned sausage slices. Heat thoroughly. Remove and discard the bay leaf. Serve in soup bowls, garnished with green onion.

Oxtail and Bean Soup

This soup shows more than a nod to Old Europe, where no part of any edible animal was allowed to go to waste. As a basic recipe, it made the crossing via the slave trade in the Caribbean. The combination of flavorful meat with affordable beans for bulk makes this a delicious, economical standby.

Serves 6

2 pounds oxtails, cut into pieces at the joints, washed and dried

¹/₄ cup vegetable oil

2 medium tomatoes, chopped

2 medium onions, chopped

1 medium green bell pepper, chopped

2 stalks celery, chopped

4 cloves garlic, minced

¹/₂ teaspoon dried thyme

1 tablespoon Creole seasoning (page 34)

6 cups water

2 cups cooked fava or navy beans

In a large stockpot or soup kettle, brown the oxtail pieces in the oil over medium heat for about 10 minutes. Add the tomatoes, onions, bell pepper, celery, garlic, thyme, and Creole seasoning and cook, stirring, until the vegetables are softened, about 10 minutes. Add 5 cups of the water and bring to a boil over high heat. Reduce the heat and simmer until the meat is tender, about 1 hour. Add the beans and the remaining 1 cup water and cook over medium heat for about 10 minutes. Serve in soup bowls.

Crawfish and Corn Bisque

Here's a bisque that's a bit more in the classic French mode, given lushness by the famed one-two punch of butter and cream. The crawfish and corn do manage, though, to turn a fairly traditional presentation into a new taste and texture sensation you'll want again and again.

Serves 8

12 ears corn

1 cup unsalted butter

2 cups chopped onion

2 cups chopped celery

1 cup tomato paste

8 cups chicken stock (page 32)

4 cups whole milk

1 tablespoon ground white pepper

1 tablespoon salt

3 pounds peeled crawfish tails

1 tablespoon Louisiana hot sauce

1/2 cup light brown roux (page 29)

8 cups heavy cream

Salt and ground black pepper

1 cup finely chopped green onion, both white and green parts

Cut the corn kernels from the cobs and set aside. Melt the butter in a large soup pot over medium-high heat. Sauté the onion and celery until the onion is opaque, about 10 minutes. Add the tomato paste and continue cooking until it begins to brown, about 5 minutes. Stir continuously to prevent sticking. Add the stock and corn. Bring to a boil and cook for about 15 minutes. Lower the heat to a simmer and add the milk, white pepper, salt, crawfish, and hot sauce. Add the cream, and simmer for 10 minutes. Season with salt and black pepper to taste and stir in the green onion. Serve in soup bowls.

Creole Crab Bisque

If you ask me or most of my family, this is a fishing camp dish that moved uptown. It's a great way to use what we call "gumbo crabs"—blue crabs that are considered too small or that have too little fat to be picked for boiling. But make no mistake: as this bisque proves, gumbo crabs are no slouches when it comes to intense crab flavor.

Serves 8

1/4 cup unsalted butter

2 bay leaves

1 cup chopped onion

1 cup chopped celery

1/2 cup chopped green bell pepper

1 cup dark brown roux (page 29)

4 quarts crab stock (page 30)

6 pounds small gumbo crabs

1 teaspoon Louisiana hot sauce

1 teaspoon Worcestershire sauce

1/2 teaspoon ground allspice

2 teaspoons ground black pepper

1/2 teaspoon cayenne pepper

2 teaspoons salt

1 pound lump crabmeat

In a large stockpot over medium-high heat, melt the butter. Sauté the bay leaves, onion, celery, and bell pepper until the onion is opaque, about 10 minutes. Stir in the roux and add the stock, a little bit at a time, stirring after each addition to fully incorporate the roux into the stock. Add the gumbo crabs and cook until they turn orange, about 5 minutes. Add the hot sauce, Worcestershire sauce, allspice, black pepper, cayenne pepper, and salt. Lower the heat, gently add the crabmeat, and simmer for 5 minutes. Remove and discard the bay leaves. Serve in soup bowls.

Crab and Corn Chowder

Corn turns up all over the cooking of south Louisiana—that means it's a flavor we truly love. When the crabs are running anywhere along our long stretches of coastline, you can bet people are using up plenty of corn in pursuit of this chowder.

Serves 6

1/4 cup unsalted butter

2 cups chopped celery

2 cups chopped onion

4 (15-ounce) cans whole-kernel corn, with liquid

2 large baking potatoes, peeled and diced

8 cups milk

4 cups heavy cream

1 pound claw crabmeat

3/4 teaspoon cayenne pepper

1/2 cup finely chopped fresh parsley

1/2 cup light brown roux (page 29)

In a medium-sized stockpot, melt the butter over medium-high heat. Sauté the celery and onion until they are opaque, about 10 minutes. Add the corn with liquid and the potatoes. Cook until the potatoes are tender, about 15 minutes. Add the milk, cream, crabmeat, cayenne pepper, and parsley. Bring to a boil, lower the heat to a simmer, and continue to simmer for 10 minutes. Add the roux and simmer until the chowder has thickened, another 10 minutes. Serve in soup bowls.

Shrimp and Corn Soup

Shrimp clearly doesn't want crabmeat to have all the fun when it comes to dressing up a basic corn soup. And since shrimp, crabmeat, or crawfish are almost always available in and around New Orleans, you can let what's fresh dictate what goes into this soup.

Serves 6

3 tablespoons vegetable oil

3 tablespoons all-purpose flour

1 medium onion, chopped

1 medium green bell pepper, chopped

2 stalks celery, chopped

1 (8-ounce) can creamed corn

3 tablespoons tomato paste

6 cups shrimp stock (page 30)

Salt and ground black pepper

1 pound medium (31/35) shrimp,
    peeled and deveined

Make a roux by heating the oil in a soup pot over medium heat, then stirring in the flour. Cook, stirring, until golden brown (see page 29). Add the onion, bell pepper, and celery, cooking until the vegetables are softened, about 10 minutes. Add the corn, tomato paste, and shrimp stock. Simmer for about 30 minutes to let the flavors blend. Season to taste with salt and pepper. Add the shrimp and cook just until they turn pink, about 10 minutes. Serve in soup bowls.

Oyster Artichoke Soup

No one should prepare this phenomenal soup without thinking of one super-talented chef, the late Warren LeRuth. Warren revolutionized the way a lot of diners looked at food in New Orleans—and he taught any chef smart enough to listen a lifetime's worth of lessons about good taste. This soup is one of his legacies.

Serves 6

12 to 15 fresh oysters

2 tablespoons unsalted butter

2 tablespoons all-puropse flour

2 cups whole milk

1 cup heavy cream

1 cup quartered canned artichoke hearts

1 teaspoon salt

1/2 teaspoon ground white pepper

1/2 teaspoon finely chopped fresh parsley

1/2 teaspoon dried tarragon

2 dashes Louisiana hot sauce

Salt and ground black pepper

1/2 cup chopped green onion, both white and green parts, for garnish

Shuck the oysters, reserving 1/2 cup oyster water (see page 23). In a medium stockpot, melt the butter over medium-high heat. Whisk in the flour and cook, whisking, for about 10 minutes to make a light brown roux (see page 29). Whisk in the milk and cream. Cook until thick, about 7 minutes. Add the artichokes, reserved oyster water, salt, white pepper, parsley, tarragon, and hot sauce. Heat until the broth is hot, then add the oysters and cook just until they curl, 8 to 10 minutes. Season to taste with salt and black pepper and serve in soup bowls, garnished with green onion.

Oyster Bisque

New Orleans cooks have a thousand ways to turn fresh oysters into bowl food. This lightly roux-thickened bisque is one of the best, a fancy restaurant classic that anyone can make at home.

....

Serves 6

¹/₂ **pint fresh oysters**

¹/₂ **cup water**

2 **tablespoons unsalted butter, at room temperature**

1¹/₂ **tablespoons all-purpose flour**

¹/₂ **teaspoon salt**

¹/₄ **teaspoon cayenne pepper**

1 **teaspoon Creole seasoning (page 34)**

2 **tablespoon chopped fresh parsley**

1 **cup heavy cream**

1 **cup whole milk**

1 **egg yolk, beaten**

¹/₄ **cup chopped green onion, both white and green parts, for garnish**

Shuck the oysters, reserving the oyster water (see page 23). In a large stockpot, bring the reserved oyster water and the water to a boil.

In the meantime, in a small sauté pan combine the butter and flour and cook, stirring, over medium heat to make a light brown roux (see page 29). Remove the pan from the heat. Season the oyster water with salt, cayenne pepper, and Creole seasoning. Add the roux to the oyster water and stir. Add the cream, milk, and egg yolk, continuing to stir. Add the oysters. Bring to a boil and lower the heat to a simmer. Cook the pot just until the edges of the oysters curl, about 8 to 10 minutes. Serve in soup bowls, garnished with green onion.

Lentil Soup with Tasso

The Cajun country ham called tasso is the flavor key in this lentil soup, with both the spice and the subtle smokiness setting this variation apart from lentil soups found anywhere else.

Serves 8 to 10

1/4 cup olive oil

1/4 cup chopped garlic

1 cup chopped onion

1 cup chopped celery

1 cup finely chopped tasso

8 quarts chicken stock (page 32)

1 pound brown lentils

3 bay leaves

2 tablespoons salt

1 tablespoon Louisiana hot sauce

1/2 cup chopped green onion, both
    white and green parts, for garnish

In a large soup pot, heat the olive oil over medium-high heat. Sauté the garlic, onion, and celery until the onion is opaque, about 10 minutes. Add the tasso and continue to sauté for 10 minutes. Add the stock, lentils, bay leaves, salt, and hot sauce. Bring to a boil, lower the heat and simmer, covered, for about an hour. Remove the lid and simmer until the soup is reduced to 4 quarts, about 45 minutes. Remove and discard the bay leaves. Adjust the seasoning and serve hot, garnished with green onion.

Black-Eyed Pea Soup

Here's a soup that is very popular as each old year fades into the new one. The notion that black-eyed peas bring good fortune is as old as the hills—or, around New Orleans, as old as the bayous. And now that Louisiana has a state lottery, off-track-betting, and a full flush of casinos, who wants to take any chances?

Serves 6 to 8

2 cups dried black-eyed peas

1 smoked ham hock

2 onions, coarsely chopped

2 carrots, peeled and coarsely chopped

1 stalk celery, with leaves

1 clove garlic, crushed

1 bay leaf

1/2 teaspoon crushed rosemary

1 teaspoon Creole seasoning (page 34)

2 jalapeño peppers, seeded and
    chopped

1/2 pound andouille or other smoked
    sausage, sliced

Wash the peas of any grit, then place them in a medium bowl, cover with several inches of water, and allow them to soak overnight. Drain the peas, reserving the liquid. Pour this liquid into a stockpot and add the ham hock, onions, carrots, celery, garlic, bay leaf, rosemary, Creole seasoning, and jalapeños. Bring the liquid to a boil, lower the heat, and simmer for 45 minutes. Strain and discard the vegetables, then skim off the fat. Return the broth and the ham hock to the heat and add the soaked peas. Simmer until the peas are tender, about 2 hours. Purée the peas in a food processor fitted with a steel blade, then return the purée to the soup. Add the smoked sausage and heat thoroughly. Serve in soup bowls.

Seafood

IF YOU TAKE ON THE JOB OF KEEPING BOWLS filled around New Orleans, you should know that our seafood is the single best place to start. In this case, it's geography that rules. Here we are, barely clinging to land that seems reclaimed from the Gulf of Mexico—and seems equally ready to silently slip right back in. You don't travel long across the marshes of south Louisiana before the billowing marsh grass blends with the sunny gray-green of lakes and bays, which in turn blends with the sky that reaches down to touch them both. It's water, water everywhere. Really. And while the old-timers may grouse about how things used to be better, the water you find in south Louisiana is full of unbelievable seafood.

In New Orleans cooking, it's worth knowing that the bulk of seafood comes from salt water. For the most part, Louisiana is a saltwater kind of place—which makes it savory, big of flavor, and kind of rowdy in the way that seaports are always rowdy. There is fresh water in the state, and more than a few bass fishermen determined to track it down. But bass figures in not a single famous New Orleans dish.

Great bowl dishes from New Orleans can and do feature all the best finfish:

redfish (red drum), speckled trout (not a true trout, but actually spotted weakfish), several forms of snapper, the flat flounder we find right along the beach, and even tuna (which no one even spotted in these waters until about fifteen years ago). In addition, the state fields a shellfish team that can't be beat: crabs pulled from the Gulf and its numberless inlets, oysters harvested from leased beds, shrimp pulled up by the ton in season, and, of course, crawfish.

Crawfish used to be a "wild" item, taken from muddy crawfish "holes" in the Atchafalaya Basin west of Baton Rouge, from specific places with revered names like Belle River. Today, most Louisiana crawfish are farmed, taking on size and good taste in the same flooded fields that give us Louisiana rice. How convenient can you get? If somebody would just build a brewery nearby, we'd have everything necessary to support life. . . .

Shrimp Creole

The Spaniards introduced tomatoes to this part of the world, just as they introduced the notion of Creole (criollo) as a New World outcropping of European stock. Around New Orleans, just about any dish with "Creole" in its name will be served in a rich tomato sauce.

Serves 8

1 cup unsalted butter

3 green bell peppers, julienned

3 onions, julienned

1/4 cup all-purpose flour

2 cups canned plum tomatoes with their juice, crushed

4 cups chicken stock (page 32)

1 cup tomato juice

1 tablespoon chopped fresh parsley

1 tablespoon Italian seasoning

1 teaspoon ground black pepper

1 teaspoon paprika

1 teaspoon Louisiana hot sauce

1/4 cup dry sherry

2 pounds peeled and deveined extra-large (16/20) shrimp

4 cups cooked white rice

In a large saucepan, melt the butter over medium-high heat. Sauté the bell peppers and onions until limp, about 10 minutes. Add the flour, stir thoroughly, and continue to cook and stir until the flour browns, about 3 minutes. Add the tomatoes, chicken stock, tomato juice, parsley, Italian seasoning, pepper, paprika, hot sauce, and sherry. Bring to a boil and lower the heat to a simmer. Simmer for 30 minutes. Add the shrimp and cook until they are pink, 5 to 7 minutes. Serve in bowls over rice.

Shrimp Stew

Without the tomatoes, shrimp Creole becomes shrimp stew—a dish more likely to turn up in the country than in the city. The deep, rich, nutty flavor supplied by the roux is sure to delight you.

....

Serves 4 to 6

3 tablespoons vegetable oil

3 tablespoons all-purpose flour

1 onion, chopped

1 green bell pepper, chopped

2 stalks celery, chopped

**1½ cups seafood stock (page 30 or 31)
   or water**

**3 pounds medium (31/35) shrimp,
   peeled and deveined**

4 cloves garlic, minced

**½ tablespoon Creole seasoning
   (page 34)**

4 hard-cooked eggs, sliced

2 or 3 cups cooked white rice

Heat the oil in a large pot over medium-high heat. Add the flour and cook, stirring, to produce a golden brown roux (see page 29). Add the onion, bell pepper, and celery, cooking until the vegetables are softened, about 10 minutes. Add the seafood stock and bring to a low boil, then add the shrimp, garlic, and Creole seasoning. Cover and simmer for 30 minutes. Add the sliced eggs to the stew and serve in bowls over rice.

Shrimp and Okra Stew

The shrimp so essential to this stew are from the Gulf, but the style of using tomatoes is from Sicily, and the notion of thickening with okra is from Africa. Prepared this way, this is "stretch food" at its finest—an old-fashioned way of feeding a lot of people for a little bit of money. If you want to take this recipe uptown a little, you have my permission to add slices of some spicy smoked sausage, like Louisiana andouille.

Serves 8 to 10

2 cups unsalted butter

2 cups chopped onion

2 cups chopped celery

2 cups chopped green bell pepper

1/2 cup chopped garlic

1 cup chopped green onion, both white and green parts

1 cup chopped fresh parsley

2 pounds okra, sliced

4 bay leaves

3 tablespoons salt

2 tablespoons coarsely ground black pepper

2 tablespoons dried thyme

1 tablespoon dried basil

1 tablespoon Creole seasoning (page 34)

1/4 cup Louisiana hot sauce

3 (15-ounce) cans plum tomatoes, with their juice

3 pounds peeled and deveined extra-large (16/20) shrimp

4 or 5 cups cooked white rice

In a large saucepan over medium-high heat, melt the butter. Sauté the onion, celery, bell pepper, and garlic until the onion is opaque, about 10 minutes. Add the green onion, parsley, okra, bay leaves, salt, pepper, thyme, basil, Creole seasoning, hot sauce, and tomatoes with juice. Bring to a boil, lower the heat to a simmer, and cook until the okra is soft, about 20 minutes. Add the shrimp and continue cooking until the shrimp is done, 10 more minutes. Remove and discard the bay leaves. Serve in bowls over rice.

BBQ Shrimp

We get a little tired of explaining to our visitors that BBQ shrimp aren't really barbecued at all. Somehow the folks who came up with this very Sicilian dish full of butter and black pepper just called it what they called it, and we've been explaining ever since. The good news is that once you start eating this messy shrimp and sopping up the sauce with every piece of French bread you can beg, borrow, or steal, your mouth will be way too full to ask any questions.

Serves 6

2 cups unsalted butter

15 cloves garlic, peeled

3 pounds head-on unpeeled extra-large (16/20) or larger shrimp

1½ cups Chablis or dry white wine

1 tablespoon Italian seasoning

3 tablespoons coarsely ground black pepper

1 tablespoon salt

¾ cup Worcestershire sauce

¼ cup Louisiana hot sauce

French bread

In a large saucepan, melt the butter over medium heat. Sauté the whole garlic cloves until the garlic begins to soften and the aroma is intense, 8 to 10 minutes. Add the shrimp, wine, Italian seasoning, pepper, salt, Worcestershire sauce, and hot sauce. Raise the heat slightly. Cook, stirring constantly, until all the shrimp are pink, about 10 minutes. Remove from the heat, cover, and let sit for 20 to 30 minutes to allow the flavors to seep into the shrimp. Reheat before serving if necessary. Serve with plenty of crusty French bread to dip in the sauce.

Navy Beans and Shrimp

With all the salt and brackish water surrounding New Orleans, it was only a matter of time before someone decided to try seasoning beans with shrimp. Bacon deliciously fills in for the traditional pickled pork or ham hocks.

Serves 8

1 pound navy beans
1 cup unsalted butter
1 cup finely chopped onion
6 slices bacon, finely chopped
8 cups water
3 bay leaves
1 teaspoon salt
1 tablespoon ground black pepper
2 tablespoons Louisiana hot sauce
1 pound peeled and deveined extra-large (16/20) shrimp
4 cups cooked white rice

Place the beans in a medium-sized bowl, cover with water, and soak overnight. Drain, rinse with fresh water, and pick out any beans that are bad. Set aside.

In a 8-quart stockpot, melt the butter over medium-high heat. Sauté the onion and bacon until the onion is opaque and the bacon is cooked, about 10 minutes. Add the water, bay leaves, salt, pepper, and hot sauce. Bring to a boil, lower the heat, and simmer until the beans are tender, about 2 hours. Add more water if necessary to prevent sticking during the cooking process. When the beans are tender, add the peeled shrimp and cook for another 20 minutes. Remove and discard the bay leaves. Serve in bowls over rice.

Crawfish Stew

When the crawfish are coming in, delicious and cheap from the Atchafalaya Basin, all of the recipes devoted to other seafoods during other seasons of the year become crawfish recipes. The fat found between the meat and the shells of the crawfish gives this dish a completely different taste from the same stew made with shrimp.

Serves 4

1/2 cup all-purpose flour

1/2 cup vegetable oil

2 medium onions, chopped

1 medium green bell pepper, chopped

1 stalk celery, chopped

3 cloves garlic, minced

1/4 cup chopped fresh parsley

1 teaspoon Creole seasoning (page 34)

2 cups seafood stock (page 30 or 31)

2 pounds peeled crawfish tails,
   with fat

2 cups cooked white rice

Make a medium brown roux by stirring the flour with the oil in a skillet or saucepan over medium-high heat, until the mixture is the color of peanut butter (see page 29). Add the onions, bell pepper, celery, garlic, parsley, and Creole seasoning and cook, stirring, until the vegetables are softened, about 10 minutes. Add the stock, bring to a boil, and lower the heat. Cover and simmer for 1 hour. Add the crawfish tails and simmer, uncovered, for about 20 minutes more, adding more stock or water if the broth gets too thick. Serve in bowls over white rice.

Crabmeat and Mirliton Maque Choux

When the local blue crabs are fat, everybody in and around New Orleans incorporates crabmeat into all their favorite recipes—when, that is, they're not just picking boiled crabs on newspaper in their driveways and backyards. Here's a different spin on the famed Cajun corn dish, combining crabmeat (lump, if possible) with not only corn but diced mirliton.

Serves 6

¼ cup unsalted butter

Kernels from 3 ears of corn

3 mirlitons (chayotes), cooked, peeled, and diced

1 medium onion, chopped

1 medium green bell pepper, chopped

2 stalks celery, chopped

2 cloves garlic, minced

1 tablespoon Creole seasoning (page 34)

1 (10-ounce) can Ro-Tel tomatoes or 3 medium tomatoes, chopped

2 cups heavy cream

1 pound crabmeat

3 cups cooked white rice

¼ cup chopped green onion, both white and green parts, for garnish

Melt the butter in a large pot over medium heat and stir in the corn kernels, cooking for about 10 minutes. Add the mirlitons, let them cook for 5 minutes, then add the onion, bell pepper, celery, and garlic. Stir over medium heat for 5 minutes, then add the Creole seasoning and tomatoes. Cook until the liquid has evaporated, about 10 minutes. Stir in the cream and bring to a boil. Lower the heat and gently fold in the crabmeat, being careful not to break up the lumps. Simmer until the cream thickens slightly, about 10 minutes. Serve in bowls over rice, garnished with green onion.

Oyster Spaghetti

The Croatian families who lived in the little bayou villages and went out each day on luggers to bring back fresh oysters from their leases loved this kind of dish. In fact, Croatian friends of mine say that during the Great Depression, almost every meal they cooked was built around oysters. It was the one thing they didn't have to pay money for! The light red sauce is a reminder that Croatia looks right across the Adriatic at Italy.

Serves 8

2 tablespoons olive oil

1 tablespoon chopped garlic

1 cup chopped onion

1 tablespoon tomato paste

1 cup dry white wine

3 cups tomato sauce

2 cups chopped plum tomatoes

2 cups oyster water (page 23) or clam juice

1 cup clam juice

1 tablespoon dried oregano

1 teaspoon ground black pepper

1 tablespoon Worcestershire sauce

1 teaspoon sugar

1/2 teaspoon Louisiana hot sauce

4 cups chopped oysters

1 cup chopped green onion, both white and green parts

2 tablespoons chopped fresh parsley

Salt

Cooked spaghetti (1 pound, cooked in 4 quarts water, for 8 to 9 minutes)

In a large sauté pan, heat the olive oil over medium heat. Sauté the garlic until it begins to brown, about 5 minutes. Add the onion and sauté until opaque, 5 to 7 minutes. Add the tomato paste, and continue to cook until it turns a brownish color, about 2 minutes. Add 1/2 cup of the wine and mix well. Add the tomato sauce, tomatoes, remaining 1/2 cup wine, oyster water, and clam juice. Bring to a boil and continue cooking until the liquid is reduced by half, about 20 minutes. Add the oregano, pepper, Worcestershire sauce, sugar, hot sauce, oysters, green onion, and parsley. Bring to a boil, lower the heat to a simmer, and cook for another 20 minutes. Adjust the salt to taste. Serve in bowls over spaghetti.

Alligator Sauce Piquante

There was a time when alligators were endangered around south Louisiana, but now they have a hunting season. They certainly are the stars of all those "Cajun swamp tours" that have become the rage around here in recent years. As for this recipe, piquante *(it's French for what the Spanish call picante) means peppery or spicy. The presentation is great with 'gator, of course, but it's also good made with chicken, fish, shrimp, sausage, or just about anything else you can think of.*

Serves 6 to 8

1/4 cup extra virgin olive oil

2 tablespoons chopped jalapeño peppers

1/3 cup chopped garlic

2 cups chopped green bell pepper

1/3 cup tomato paste

2 cups canned tomatoes, puréed in a blender

1 (46-ounce) can tomato juice

1 tablespoon ground cumin

1 tablespoon chile powder

1 pound boiled and cubed alligator fillet

1 pound boiled and sliced alligator sausage

Salt and ground black pepper

3 or 4 cups cooked white rice

Heat the olive oil in a medium sauté pan over high heat. Sauté the jalapeños, garlic, and bell pepper for about 5 minutes Add the tomato paste and sauté for 2 minutes. Add the tomatoes, tomato juice, cumin, chile powder, and alligator fillet and sausage. Bring to a boil, lower the heat to a simmer, and cook for 30 minutes. Season to taste with salt and pepper and serve in bowls over rice.

Frog Legs Sauce Piquante

We can't speak for everybody else, but in New Orleans we treat frog legs like seafood. The flavor of the meat (despite the standard comparison to chicken) can be quite a lot like mild, white-fleshed fish. Besides, we have lots of frogs in south Louisiana—and lots of recipes left over from our days as a French colony. This is one of our favorites from the Creole-Cajun repertoire

Serves 10

1 cup vegetable oil

3 tablespoons all-purpose flour

4 medium onions, chopped

6 cloves garlic, minced

1 stalk celery, chopped

1 (28-ounce) can chopped tomatoes, drained and juice reserved, or 5 medium tomatoes, chopped

1 (10-ounce) can Ro-Tel tomatoes, drained and juice reserved, or 3 medium tomatoes, chopped

1 or 2 teaspoons Creole seasoning (page 34)

12 medium frog legs

1 cup seafood stock (page 30 or 31) or water

5 cups cooked white rice

Make a dark brown roux in a Dutch oven or large, heavy saucepan by stirring the oil and flour together over medium-high heat until a dark brown color is achieved (see page 29). Add the onions, garlic, and celery and cook, stirring, until softened, 8 to 10 minutes. Add both kinds of tomatoes and cook for 5 more minutes. Add the juice from the tomatoes and the Creole seasoning. Add the frog legs and the stock. Simmer, covered, for about 4 hours. Serve in bowls over rice.

Poultry, Meat, and Game

DESPITE THE PROXIMITY OF BAYOUS AND BAYS, you'd be wrong to think that New Orleans lives by seafood alone. There are just too many ethnic traditions colliding in this crazy melting pot not to have a meat tradition that's almost the equal of our seafood tradition. The thing to remember about New Orleans meat cookery, though, is that the whole idea is to get a lot from a little. Generally, when we talk about meat dishes, especially ones destined for a bowl, we're talking about cheap cuts that need to be cooked long and slow for tenderness, simmered with vegetables in a generous sauce, and then ladled over mountains of white rice.

One word really stands out if you want to cook meat New Orleans style: smothered. This is one of several variations of braising embraced in these parts as a way to slow-cook less than stellar cuts until you can bite through them. Smothered meats range from pork chops to that unforgettable Creole classic grillades and grits, the latter made with either beef or veal simmered in a spicy, tomato-kissed gravy and served not with rice (for a change) but with buttered grits borrowed from the breakfast table.

Grillades and Grits

This is the brunch dish to end all brunch dishes in the city that probably invented brunch—though New Orleans' legendary cook Madame Begue called the meal "second breakfast" instead. We're basically okay with either name, especially when it promises foods like these beef rounds smothered in reddish brown gravy and served over a mound of hot, delicious, Deep South grits. Rumored to cure hangovers, this is hearty morning fare.

Serves 6 to 8

2 tablespoons all-purpose flour

6 to 8 boneless beef round steaks (5 to 6 ounces each), trimmed of excess fat and cut into serving pieces

2 tablespoons vegetable oil

1 large red onion, finely chopped

1 green bell pepper, finely chopped

2 stalks celery, finely chopped

3 cloves garlic, minced

2 bay leaves

2 teaspoons chopped fresh parsley

1 (8-ounce) can tomato sauce

4 cups beef stock (page 32)

1 tablespoon Creole seasoning (page 34)

Salt and ground black pepper

4 cups hot cooked grits

In a large, cast-iron skillet, heat the oil and brown the beef on all sides over medium-high heat, then remove it from the pan. Stir in the flour and cook, stirring, over medium-high heat to make a dark brown roux (see page 29). Add the onion, bell pepper, celery, garlic, bay leaves, and parsley and cook, stirring, until the vegetables are softened. Add the tomato sauce, beef stock, and Creole seasoning. Season with salt and pepper. Bring to a boil, lower the heat, and simmer for 10 minutes to let the flavors blend, then return the meat to the pan and simmer until it is tender, 35 to 40 minutes. Remove and discard the bay leaves. Serve in bowls over hot grits.

Rabbit Sauce Piquante

Out in the fields of south Louisiana, all references to cute (or even smart-mouthed) cartoon characters are forgotten and rabbit becomes a delicious white meat a hunter can put on the table. There are some terrific rabbit stews among the country classics of France, Spain, and Italy. This dish may well borrow something from each of them.

Serves 8

2 small rabbits, cut into small serving
    pieces
2 tablespoons prepared Creole
    mustard
1 tablespoon Worcestershire sauce
1/4 cup all-purpose flour
1/4 cup vegetable oil
3 cloves garlic, chopped
4 medium onions, chopped
3 green bell peppers, chopped
3 stalks celery, chopped
1 lemon, quartered
2 bay leaves
1 cup sliced fresh mushrooms
2 (8-ounce) cans tomato sauce
3/4 cup dry red wine
1 tablespoon Creole seasoning
    (page 34)
Salt and ground black pepper
4 cups cooked white rice

Marinate the rabbits in a mixture of the mustard and Worcestershire sauce for 1 to 2 hours. In a large skillet, stir together the flour and oil. Cook, stirring, over medium-high heat to make a medium brown roux (see page 29). Add the garlic, onions, bell peppers, and celery to the roux, stirring until the vegetables are softened, about 10 minutes. Squeeze the lemon juice into the skillet, then add the rind. Add the bay leaves, mushrooms, tomato sauce, red wine, and Creole seasoning. Season to taste with salt and pepper. Simmer for 2 to 3 hours, until the rabbit is tender. Remove and discard the bay leaves and lemon rinds. Serve in bowls over rice.

Rabbit Dirty Rice

The addition of duck or chicken livers to the mild, white rabbit meat makes for a flavor that the city that loves dirty rice just has to adore. And there's a dark brown roux to make sure the color is "dirty" enough for anybody's taste.

....

Serves 8

1/4 cup vegetable oil

1 pound boneless rabbit meat, finely chopped

1/2 pound duck or chicken livers, finely chopped

1 medium onion, chopped

1 small green bell pepper, chopped

4 cloves garlic, minced

2 teaspoons Creole seasoning (page 34)

2 cups chicken stock (page 32)

1/4 cup dark brown roux (page 29)

4 cups cooked white rice

1/2 cup chopped green onion, both white and green parts

Heat the oil in a large cast-iron skillet over medium heat. Brown the rabbit and liver for about 10 minutes, scraping the bottom of the pan often to prevent sticking. Add the onion, bell pepper, garlic, Creole seasoning, and chicken stock. Bring the mixture to a boil and cook for 5 minutes. Stir in the roux, lower the heat, and simmer for 20 minutes. Remove the skillet from the heat and fold in the cooked rice and green onion. Serve in bowls.

Deer-Season Stew

In the wintertime, when so many New Orleans doctors, lawyers, and engineers turn into gun-toting hunters every weekend, you or someone you know may well bring home some venison. And there's usually plenty of meat to go around. Browning the venison in the bacon drippings gives a flavor that lasts all the way to the dinner table.

....

Serves 10

1/2 **pound bacon, cut into 1-inch dice**

2 **pounds venison, cut into bite-sized pieces**

1 **tablespoon Creole seasoning (page 34)**

1/4 **cup all-purpose flour**

1 **medium onion, chopped**

1 **medium green bell pepper, chopped**

2 **stalks celery, chopped**

1 **large tomato, chopped**

4 **cloves garlic, minced**

6 **cups venison stock (page 33)**

2 **medium potatoes, peeled and cut into 1-inch cubes**

5 **cups cooked white rice**

1 **tablespoon chopped fresh parsley, for garnish**

Brown the bacon in a deep, heavy skillet or saucepan over medium-high heat. Remove the bacon, leaving about 1/4 cup of drippings and adding a little vegetable oil if necessary. Sprinkle the venison with the Creole seasoning and flour. Brown the meat in the bacon drippings for about 5 minutes. Add the onion, bell pepper, celery, tomato, and garlic, stirring until the vegetables are softened, about 10 minutes. Add the stock, bring to a boil, reduce the heat, and simmer, covered, for about 1 hour. Add the potatoes and simmer until they are cooked, about 15 minutes more. Serve the stew in bowls over rice, garnished with chopped parsley and crumbled bacon.

Turtle Stew

Here's a rustic turn on the refined turtle soup devoured each night in the French Quarter's Creole palaces. It's the kind of wonderful country dish that you might smell cooking in the back of those falling-down stores where turtle meat is often sold.

....

Serves 8

3 pounds turtle meat

3 tablespoons vegetable oil

3 tablespoons all-purpose flour

2 medium onions, chopped

3 cloves garlic, minced

2 tomatoes, chopped

1 (6-ounce) can tomato paste

8 green onions, both white and green
    parts, chopped

2 stalks celery, finely chopped

2 green bell peppers, finely chopped

1 cup dry sherry

1 or 2 tablespoons Creole seasoning
    (page 34)

4 bay leaves

4 whole cloves

1/2 teaspoon ground allspice

1 tablespoon sugar

6 hard-boiled eggs

1/4 cup unsalted butter

1 lemon, sliced

4 cups cooked white rice

Bring a large pot of salted water to a boil. Chop the turtle meat into bite-sized pieces, add to the water, and cook for 10 to 15 minutes. Drain and reserve the turtle meat, discarding the cooking liquid. In a large stewpot, stir together the oil and flour. Cook, stirring, over medium-high heat to produce a dark brown roux (see page 29). Add the onions, garlic, tomatoes, and tomato paste, cooking over low heat for about 20 minutes. Return the turtle meat to the pot, along with enough boiling water to cover it. Add the green onions, celery, bell peppers, sherry, Creole seasoning, bay leaves, cloves, allspice, and sugar. Cover and cook for 30 minutes. Mash the egg yolks and chop the whites, adding both to the stew to help thicken it. Cover and cook over low heat for 2 hours. Stir in the butter and lemon slices and cook until the turtle meat is tender, about 1 hour more. Remove and discard the bay leaves, whole spices, and lemon rinds. Serve in bowls over rice.

Smothered Quail

Although quail have a past among south Louisiana hunters, today's quail is usuully farm-raised, milder in flavor than wild quail, and more likely to be available every day of the year. Quail are terrific simply roasted with a sprinkle of salt and pepper, but we also love this version, with the pieces cut up and slow-cooked in a lush gravy.

....

Serves 6 to 8

1/4 cup Creole seasoning (page 34)

12 quail, cut into serving pieces

1 1/2 cups all-purpose flour

1/2 cup vegetable oil

3 medium onions, chopped

2 medium green bell peppers, chopped

2 stalks celery, chopped

4 cloves garlic, minced

1 cup chicken stock (page 32)

3 or 4 cups cooked white rice

1 cup chopped green onion, both white and green parts, for garnish

Sprinkle the Creole seasoning over the quail pieces. Place the flour on a large plate or pie pan and dredge the quail in the flour, shaking off any excess. Heat the oil in a large, heavy pot over medium-high heat, and brown the quail on all sides. Remove the quail and discard all but about 1 tablespoon of the oil. Sauté the onions, bell peppers, celery, and garlic until softened, about 8 minutes, then return the quail to the pot and pour in the stock. Turn the heat down to low and cover the pot. Cook the quail until the meat is very tender and a thick gravy forms, about 45 minutes. Serve in bowls over rice, garnished with green onion.

Chicken Sauce Piquante

Creoles and Cajuns put everything else in a sauce piquante—why not chicken, one of the most familiar and accessible foods of all? The mushrooms add a nice touch to this Creole-Cajun chicken stew

Serves 6

1 large fryer (3½ pounds), cut into small serving pieces

1 tablespoon Creole seasoning (page 34)

½ cup vegetable oil

½ cup all-purpose flour

2 medium onions, chopped

2 medium green bell peppers, chopped

3 stalks celery, chopped

4 cloves garlic, minced

1 (8-ounce) can tomato sauce

1 (10-ounce) can whole tomatoes, with their juice

3 bay leaves

1 cup sliced fresh mushrooms

¼ cup chopped green onion, both white and green parts

¼ cup chopped fresh parsley

1 teaspoon Louisiana hot sauce

3 cups cooked white rice

Season the chicken pieces with the Creole seasoning, then heat the oil in a heavy skillet over medium-high heat and brown the chicken rapidly. Remove the chicken pieces and stir the flour into the oil. Cook, stirring, until you've made a dark brown roux (see page 29). Add the onions, bell peppers, celery, and garlic and cook, stirring, until the vegetables are softened, about 10 minutes. Carefully add the tomato sauce, tomatoes, and bay leaves. Cover and simmer, stirring occasionally, for about 45 minutes. Return the chicken to the pan and simmer until it is tender, about 1 hour. Add the mushrooms, green onion, parsley, and hot sauce, and simmer 15 minutes longer. Remove and discard the bay leaves. Serve in bowls over rice.

Chicken Maque Choux

In recent years, maque choux has become popular in restaurants that shortly before had never heard of this Cajun spin on a Native American dish. A host of chef spinoffs developed quickly, including this hearty combination of chicken and fresh corn.

Serves 6 to 8

4 boneless chicken breasts, cut into bite-sized pieces

2 or 3 tablespoons Creole seasoning (page 34)

1/4 cup vegetable oil

4 cups fresh corn kernels (from about 6 ears corn)

3 tablespoons heavy cream

1 medium onion, chopped

1 small green bell pepper, chopped

2 large tomatoes, chopped

1/4 teaspoon dried thyme

1/4 teaspoon dried basil

1 tablespoon chopped fresh parsley

2 or 3 tablespoons milk

Sprinkle the chicken with Creole seasoning. Heat the oil in a large saucepan over medium heat and brown the chicken. Lower the heat and add the corn and cream, mixing thoroughly. Add the onion, bell pepper, tomatoes, thyme, basil, and parsley and cook over low heat until the chicken is very tender, about 20 minutes. Add the milk when the dish is nearly ready. Serve in bowls.

Pork Neckbones

This is definitely a dish that rich people had to learn about from poor people, and they probably felt compelled to find a new name for it somewhere along the way—preferably something French. But in the colorful if sometimes crumbling old neighborhoods of New Orleans, pork neckbones are a favorite. You'll need to start a day ahead to give the meat time to marinate.

Serves 6

2 pounds pork neckbones with meat

1 tablespoon Creole seasoning
   (page 34)

5 tablespoons vegetable oil

1 medium onion, chopped

1 medium green bell pepper, chopped

2 stalks celery, chopped

4 cloves garlic, chopped

1/4 cup chopped fresh parsley

2 tablespoons all-purpose flour

2 cups chicken stock (page 32)

Cornbread (page 140)

Season the pork neckbones with the Creole seasoning. Heat 3 tablespoons of the oil in a heavy skillet over medium-high heat, and brown the neckbones quickly, about 15 minutes. Transfer the neckbones to a bowl and cover with the onion, bell pepper, celery, garlic, and parsley. Let marinate overnight in the refrigerator.

In a large, heavy skillet over medium-high heat, stir together the flour and the remaining 2 tablespoons oil. Cook, stirring, to make a medium brown roux (see page 29). Add the chopped vegetables (but not the neckbones) and cook them in the roux until they simmer until the flavors are blended, about 15 minutes. Add the neckbones and cook over low heat until the meat is tender and the gravy has thickened, about 45 minutes. Serve in bowls with plenty of gravy over squares of cornbread.

Creole Irish Stew

Even a New Orleanian named O'Brien or O'Malley will assure you that Irish food as he knows it is bland and boring. That's why traditional dishes like Irish stew take a detour through the Creole-Cajun kitchen, showing up at the table with more depth of flavor and a surprising bit of pizzazz.

Serves 8

5 pounds boneless lamb, cut into
   1-inch cubes

8 cups water

3 large onions, chopped

2 large potatoes, peeled and chopped

4 green onions, both white and green
   parts, chopped

5 stalks celery, chopped

4 cloves garlic, chopped

1 tablespoon Creole seasoning
   (page 34)

24 pearl onions

16 new potatoes, peeled

8 carrots, peeled and sliced into
   1 1/2-inch sticks

1/4 cup chopped fresh parsley,
   for garnish

Place the lamb in a large stewpot with enough water to cover, bring to a boil, and cook for 5 minutes. Drain, discarding the water. Rinse the meat and clean the pot, then return the meat to the pot with the water. Add the chopped onions, potatoes, green onions, celery, garlic, and Creole seasoning. Bring to a boil and cook, uncovered, for 1 hour. Remove the meat from the pot. Purée the vegetables in a blender with a little water, then pour the purée back into the pot. In a separate pot, lightly boil the pearl onions, new potatoes, and carrot sticks in water to cover for about 5 minutes, then drain and add them to the vegetable purée, along with the meat. Cook the stew until all the vegetables are tender and the flavors have blended, about 30 minutes. Serve in bowls, garnished with chopped parsley.

Smothered Nutria

Some years ago, Harry Lee (the tough-talking, cowboy hat–wearing Chinese sheriff of one New Orleans suburb) offered a bounty for each of these over-multiplying swamp rats local hunters could bring in. The Louisiana Department of Agriculture had what it described as a better idea: convince the world that nutria, like soup in that TV commercial, was good food. The mission has proven a tough one, but that hasn't stopped some local chefs from giving nutria a chance. This recipe, inspired by Chef Paul Prudhomme's sister Enola, is one of the better showcases of nutria we've seen. And, if you can't get or don't want to try nutria, it also works well with rabbit or even chicken.

Serves 6

2 tablespoons vegetable oil

2 pounds cleaned boneless nutria meat, cut into bite-sized pieces

4 teaspoons Creole seasoning (page 34)

2 medium onions, chopped

1 medium green bell pepper, chopped

1 stalk celery, chopped

4 cloves garlic, minced

1 tablespoon all-purpose flour

3 3/4 cups chicken stock (page 32)

3 cups cooked white rice

1/4 cup chopped green onion, both white and green parts, for garnish

Heat the oil in a heavy 5-quart saucepan over high heat. Sprinkle the meat with Creole seasoning, then brown the pieces in the oil. Cook, stirring, for 10 minutes, then add the onions, bell pepper, celery, garlic, and flour, stirring for 10 minutes more. Carefully pour in the chicken stock, bring the liquid to a boil, lower the heat, and simmer for 15 minutes, scraping the bottom of the pot occasionally. Serve in bowls over cooked white rice, garnished with green onion.

Vegetables

NEW ORLEANIANS LOVE VEGETABLES. We love them as side dishes, just like everybody else—though often with a bit more butter, bacon grease, or spice than these "healthy" foods probably deserve. That's because in New Orleans, it's never really about health. It's always about flavor. Most of us swear off the good stuff once in a while, under pressure from our doctors. But even when we have to do it, we don't have to like it.

What might at a glance seem like a city of meats and seafoods is also a city of delectable vegetables. To start with, there's the blessed Trinity of seasoning vegetables—onion, bell pepper, and celery—which adds flavor, texture, and a little nutritional balance to almost every savory Creole or Cajun dish. And then there's our love affair with beans, often characteric in the cuisines of poor people. Red beans and rice is the "national dish" of New Orleans, filling the same place of adoration as rice and peas in the Caribbean and feijoada in Brazil. Many other beans find their way onto New Orleans tables, mostly cooked the same way as red beans: with a bit of pickled or smoked pork and a side order of andouille sausage.

With vegetable dishes often prepared in this meaty manner, no one ever accuses New Orleans veggies of being "rabbit food" (here, we're much more likely to eat a rabbit than to ever eat *like* one). But we also love vegetables as main courses. No, we're not vegetarians. Those are usually the kind of people who come here from elsewhere and complain that they can't find anything on our menus for them. We try to be friendly. We try to be nice. But the truth is, even the vegetables on our menu aren't specially made for them. They're for us.

Red Beans and Rice

It's hard to say why or how red beans and rice came to be one of the "national dishes" (or perhaps the national dish) of New Orleans. Certainly, the city's deep roots in the Caribbean taught it to appreciate dozens of variations, from rice and peas to the colorfully named moros y cristianos. *But maybe it was just that people needed something to cook on Mondays while they did their laundry. Whatever the reason, long after the city stopped agreeing that Monday was laundry day, it agrees (from the richest to the poorest quarters) that Monday is red beans and rice day.*

Serves 6 to 8

1/4 cup unsalted butter

2 tablespoons chopped garlic

1 3/4 cups chopped celery

1 1/4 cups chopped onion

1 3/4 cups chopped green bell pepper

1 pound andouille or other smoked
   sausage, thinly sliced

2 bay leaves

8 cups water

2 pounds red beans, soaked overnight

1/2 tablespoon liquid smoke

3 or 4 tablespoons Louisiana hot
   sauce

3 tablespoons Worcestershire sauce

3/4 tablespoon chile powder

Salt and ground black pepper

3 or 4 cups cooked white rice

In a large stockpot over medium heat, melt the butter. Sauté the garlic until you smell the aroma, about 2 minutes. Add the celery, onion, and bell pepper, and sauté until opaque, 8 to 10 minutes. Add the smoked sausage and continue to sauté until it's brown on the edges, 5 to 7 minutes. Add the bay leaves, water, red beans, liquid smoke, hot sauce, Worcestershire sauce, and chile powder. Bring to a boil and lower the heat to a simmer. Simmer, uncovered, for about 3 hours, or until the beans are tender. Season to taste with salt and pepper. Remove and discard the bay leaves. Serve over rice.

Maque Choux

This is often called the "famous Cajun corn dish," but the Cajuns actually learned it from the neighboring Attakapas Indians. Think about it: maque choux contains a lot more of the stuff the Indians probably brought to the first Thanksgiving than anything the Cajuns ever cooked in Nova Scotia or Louisiana. Cooked long enough, it's basically a corn pudding (see page 82 for a soupier version).

Serves 10

12 ears corn

2 tablespoons unsalted butter

1 tablespoon vegetable oil

1/2 cup chopped onion

1/2 cup chopped red bell pepper

1/2 cup chopped green bell pepper

1/2 teaspoon dried thyme

1 teaspoon salt

1 teaspoon ground white pepper

1/2 teaspoon cayenne pepper

2 cups chopped plum tomatoes

1/2 teaspoon ground black pepper

1/4 cup heavy cream

In a medium mixing bowl, cut the kernels from corn and scrape the cobs with a fork to obtain a milky pulp. You should have about 8 cups of corn.

In a large sauté pan, heat the butter and oil. Add the onion and bell peppers and sauté until opaque, 10 to 15 minutes. Add the corn, thyme, salt, and white pepper. Fry until the corn begins to stick. Add the cayenne pepper, tomatoes, black pepper, and heavy cream. Bring to a boil and lower the heat to a simmer. Cook for 10 minutes. Serve in bowls.

Okra and Tomatoes

When slaves carried the seeds to plant okra around their huts in the still-unknown New World, they surely had never heard of tomatoes—which still were generally considered poisonous in America anyway. When okra and tomatoes got together, however, one of the Deep South's simplest and best side dishes was born.

. . . .

Serves 8

1/4 cup vegetable oil
3 quarts sliced fresh okra
1 medium green bell pepper, chopped
1 large onion, chopped
2 cloves garlic, minced
3 medium tomatoes, chopped
1 or 2 tablespoons Creole seasoning
   (page 34)

Heat the oil in a heavy pot over low heat and stir in the okra, bell pepper, onion, garlic, tomatoes, and Creole seasoning. Cook, uncovered, over low heat for about 1 hour, stirring often to prevent sticking.

Butter Beans

As you can tell, we love our beans in New Orleans—and that means all our beans. Pickled pork provides a lot of the flavor here, as it does in so many Crescent City classics.

....

Serves 6 to 8

1/2 **pound large lima beans, soaked overnight**

2 **tablespoons unsalted butter**

1/2 **cup chopped onion**

1/2 **pound pickled pork (see page 23)**

1/2 **cup chopped celery**

4 **cups water**

2 **bay leaves**

1/8 **teaspoon red pepper flakes**

3/4 **tablespoon coarsely ground black pepper**

1/2 **teaspoon salt**

1/2 **tablespoon Louisiana hot sauce**

Place the beans in a large stockpot, cover with water, and bring to a boil. Remove from the heat and let sit for 1 hour. Drain, rinse, and remove any bad beans. In a medium-sized stockpot, melt the butter over medium-high heat and sauté the onion with the pickled pork until the onion is opaque, 7 to 10 minutes. Add the celery and continue to sauté for an additional 5 minutes. Add the water, beans, and bay leaves. Bring to a boil over high heat and cook for 5 to 10 minutes. Lower the heat and simmer until the beans are tender, 1 hour. Add the pepper flakes, black pepper, salt, and hot sauce and simmer for 5 minutes. Removethe bay leaves before serving.

Smothered Cabbage

Some of the best meals served in any eatery in New Orleans are prepared by the help—for the help. These staff or "family" meals tend to be soul food, and one of the best soul food dishes of all is smothered cabbage cooked just like this. It's one more reminder, as though we needed one in a city as racially and culturally tangled as New Orleans, that good-tasting food really is the great equalizer.

Serves 8

1 cup unsalted butter

2 cups chopped onion

1 cup chopped celery

2 medium-sized heads green cabbage, cored and coarsely chopped

1 tablespoon salt

½ tablespoon coarsely ground black pepper

4 cups chicken stock (page 32)

4 cups cooked white rice

In a medium-sized saucepan over medium heat, melt the butter. Add the onion and cook until caramelized, 5 to 10 minutes. Add the celery and cabbage. Toss with a spoon to coat with the onion and butter. Stir-fry over medium heat until the cabbage is lightly browned, 15 to 20 minutes. Add the salt, pepper, and stock. Reduce the heat and simmer until most of the liquid is gone and the cabbage is tender, about 30 minutes. Stir occasionally to prevent sticking. Serve over rice.

Mixed Greens

Poor people have always had a hard time affording anything but the cheapest cuts of meat to bring flavor to their greens. But this is the Deep South, and even something as otherwise unappealing as pork neck bones can do an incredible job of turning mustard and turnip greens right on their delicious ear.

Serves 4

2 bunches turnip greens

1 bunch mustard greens

2 pounds pork neck bones with meat

1/4 cup sugar

1/2 cup unsalted butter

2 cups chopped onion

6 cups water

1 teaspoon salt

1 tablespoon ground black pepper

Wash the greens, remove the center vein, and tear gently by hand. In a mixing bowl, toss the pork bones with 2 tablespoons of the sugar. In a large stockpot, melt the butter over high heat and brown the pork bones for about 10 minutes. Add the onion and sauté until opaque, 5 to 7 minutes. Add the water and bring to a boil. Add the greens, salt, and pepper. Lower the heat, cover, and simmer until tender, 1$^{1}/_{2}$ to 2 hours. Serve as a side dish.

Black-Eyed Peas

Although New Orleanians are perfectly capable of ladling black-eyed peas over rice and serving it as an entrée, they are even more likely to follow the broader Southern tradition of black-eyed peas as a side dish.

Serves 10 to 12

3 tablespoons unsalted butter

1 cup chopped green bell pepper

1 cup chopped onion

1 cup chopped celery

1 pound ham, cut into 1-inch pieces

2 pounds black-eyed peas, rinsed and picked over

8 cups water

2 bay leaves

2 tablespoons salt

2 tablespoons ground black pepper

In a large soup pot, melt the butter over medium-high heat. Sauté the bell pepper, onion, and celery until the onion is opaque, about 10 minutes. Add the ham and sauté for 2 minutes. Add the peas, water, bay leaves, salt, and pepper. Bring to a boil. Lower the heat and simmer, uncovered, for $1^1/2$ to 2 hours. Stir at intervals to keep the peas from sticking, adding more water if necessary. Remove and discard the bay leaves. Serve as a side dish.

Green Beans, Red Potatoes, and Pickled Pork

Here's a triumph of food sense over poverty, a way of stretching two vegetable side dishes into a main dish with only a little pickled pork. Time and again, this is the genius of soul food—one that taught some mighty good lessons to New Orleans cooks of every race and cultural background.

Serves 6 to 8

1 cup unsalted butter

1¹/₂ pounds pickled pork (see page 23),
    cut into ¹/₂-inch cubes

4 cups chopped onion

2¹/₂ pounds fresh green beans, cut into
    1- to 2-inch lengths, ends trimmed

2 bay leaves

4 quarts chicken stock (page 32)

1 tablespoon salt

1 tablespoon ground black pepper

3 pounds tiny red potatoes

3 or 4 cups cooked white rice

In a large soup pot, melt the butter over medium-high heat. Add the pickled pork and onion and sauté until opaque, about 10 minutes. Add the beans, bay leaves, chicken stock, salt, and pepper. Bring to a boil, lower the heat, and simmer, uncovered, for about 30 minutes. Add the potatoes, cover, and cook until the potatoes are done, another 10 to 12 minutes. Remove and discard the bay leaves. Serve as a main dish with plenty of pot liquor, with or without rice.

Beet Salad

Look just to this or that side of your Monday red beans and rice and you'll probably see some version of a beet salad. The combination must make people happy, and besides, beans always taste better with a little splash of vinegar. In this case, the splash is accidental—or is it?

Serves 8

1 pound beets
1 cup balsamic vinegar
$^1\!/_2$ cup olive oil
$^1\!/_2$ teaspoon salt
Ground black pepper

Cut off the tops and roots of the beets. Peel and rinse under cold water. Slice them in $^1\!/_4$-inch rounds. Place the beet slices in a large saucepan, cover with water, and bring to a boil. Cook until tender, about 20 minutes. Drain the beets and cool. Place the beets in a medium-sized bowl and pour the vinegar and oil over them. Season with salt and pepper to taste. Refrigerate for at least 1 hour before serving.

Candied Sweet Potato Casserole

Sweet potatoes (usually called "yams" around New Orleans) are a classic side for baked chicken—or, of course, baked turkey. But don't forget this recipe when you're looking for something to serve during duck season, especially with roast duck and oyster dressing.

Serves 6 to 8

3 pounds sweet potatoes

1/4 cup unsalted butter, at room temperature

1 tablespoon ground cinnamon

1 1/2 cups dark brown sugar

1 tablespoon grated orange zest

Preheat the oven to 350°F. Peel the sweet potatoes and cut into 1- to 1 1/2-inch cubes. Place in a large stockpot, cover with water, and bring to a boil. Cook until tender, about 30 minutes. While the potatoes are cooking, in a small mixing bowl combine the butter, cinnamon, brown sugar, and orange zest. When the potatoes are done, drain them thoroughly, return to the pot, and coat with the sugar mixture. Place the potatoes in a large glass baking dish and cover with foil. Cover and bake for 30 minutes. Serve as a side dish.

Creamed Potatoes

The cream here might be a little like gilding the lily, but it's so good you'll see why generation after generation of New Orleans mamas had a favorite recipe for this dish. It's terrific with a traditional New Orleans roast beef, sometimes called a daube.

Serves 6

2 pounds baking potatoes, about 4
  medium potatoes
$1/2$ cup unsalted butter
$1/2$ cup heavy cream
$1^1/2$ cups milk
1 teaspoon salt
1 teaspoon ground black pepper

Rinse and peel the potatoes. Cut into $1/2$-inch cubes. Place in a large stockpot, cover with water, and boil until tender, 15 to 20 minutes. Drain and place in a bowl. Fold in the butter until melted. Using a hand mixer, cream the potatoes, adding cream and milk alternately until the desired consistency is reached. Season with salt and pepper. Serve as a side dish.

Alligator Pear Salad

Whenever you hear New Orleanians talk about alligator pear, they of course mean avocado. This dish flirts with Mexican guacamole, but it goes its own way with the Sicilian blending of olive oil and red wine vinegar.

Serves 4 to 6

1 ripe avocado

1/4 cup chopped celery

1/4 cup finely chopped red onion

1 cup diced plum tomatoes (1/2-inch dice)

Juice of 1 lime

1/4 cup red wine vinegar

1/2 cup olive oil

1 tablespoon Creole seasoning (page 34)

1 head iceberg lettuce, torn by hand into pieces

Cut the avocado into quarters, remove the peel, and dice the meat into 1/2-inch pieces. Place in a mixing bowl. Add the celery, onion, and tomatoes. Squeeze the lime juice over the vegetables and mix gently. Add the vinegar, olive oil, and Creole seasoning. Chill for 1/2 hour. To serve, toss with the iceberg lettuce.

Breads

PEOPLE SAY THE ONLY SUCCESSFUL NEW ORLEANS meal is one that leaves a tableful of bread crumbs as its legacy. That, of course, refers to good, solid, satisfying New Orleans French bread, not to anything that comes in anemic white slices or barely stands up to a pat of butter. New Orleanians love their bread—and it had better be their bread, which they will then insist is better than, different from, and utterly unique among the breads found anywhere on earth. It's the Mississippi River water that does it, some will pontificate. No, it's the humidity in the air, others will counter. No, it must be some strange yeast that grows only here, still others insist, envisioning some flour-flecked version of Jurassic Park. When New Orleanians fantasize about bowl cuisine, they always fantasize about the bread beside the bowl, too.

Fact is, few New Orleanians would ever consider baking French bread. The stuff is already baked for us, it's good and cheap, and it's delivered fresh daily by a host of trucks emblazoned with beloved brands like Leidenheimer, Reising, Zip, and, in the case of restaurants, Gendusa. These bakeries, knowing what they do of the technical process, try not to support the cockeyed theories spread by uninformed zealots about why New Orleans French bread is so special. But they try not to discourage them either.

Apart from French bread and its omnipresence, from white-tablecloth restaurants to dingy po' boy joints, New Orleans has made an extra place in its heart for the heavy, crusty, Sicilian muffaletta loaf. After all, when this sandwich was invented here at the start of the twentieth century, it took its name from the traditional Sicilian bread its creators decided to build it on. And beyond French and muffaletta loaves, New Orleans is sleepy time down South. All the Deep South bread fetishes can be enjoyed here en masse, from dinner rolls to biscuits to hush puppies. Hush puppies, of course, are corn bread that's fried. How could a city like New Orleans resist?

French Bread

In New Orleans, as in France, most people don't actually bake French bread—they buy it instead. But, here's a recipe that should work for you if you're not fortunate enough to have access to a good bakery.

Makes 4 loaves

1 package active dry yeast (about 1 tablespoon)
2½ cups warm water (110°F)
2 tablespoons sugar
1 teaspoon salt
7 cups sifted all-purpose flour
2 egg whites, well beaten

In a large bowl, combine the yeast, warm water, sugar, and salt; stir until dissolved. Gradually add the flour and mix until well blended. Knead on a well-floured surface until the dough is smooth and satiny, about 10 minutes. Let the dough rise in a warm place until it doubles in bulk. Punch it down and place it on a floured surface. Knead the dough 3 or 4 times to remove any air, and divide it into 4 equal pieces.

Grease 4 standard loaf pans. Shape the dough into loaves and place in the pans. Slash the tops and brush them with the egg white. Let the loaves rise until they double in bulk. Preheat the oven to 350°F and bake for 30 minutes. Remove the bread from the pans and let cool.

Sicilian Muffaletta Loaf

The muffaletta sandwich was named after this crusty, round Sicilian bread. In New Orleans people buy muffaletta bread from their grocery store, but here's a way to whip some up anytime, anywhere.

Makes one 10-inch loaf

1 cup warm water (110°F)

1 tablespoon sugar

1 package active dry yeast (about 1 tablespoon)

About 3 cups bread flour

1¹/₂ teaspoons salt

2 tablespoons olive oil

Sesame seeds

In a 2-cup glass measuring cup, combine the water and sugar. Stir in the yeast and let stand until foamy, 5 to 10 minutes. In a large mixing bowl, combine 3 cups of the flour, the salt, and the olive oil. Add the yeast mixture. Using hands dipped regularly in warm water, knead until the dough forms a ball. If the dough is too dry, knead in more warm water, 1 tablespoon at a time. If it is too sticky, add more flour, 1 or 2 tablespoons at a time.

Lightly oil a large bowl. Place the dough in the oiled bowl; turn to coat all sides. Cover the bowl with plastic wrap. Let the dough rise in a warm, draft-free place until it doubles in bulk, about 1¹/₂ hours. Lightly grease a baking sheet. When the dough has doubled, punch it down and turn it out onto a lightly floured surface. Form the dough into a round loaf about 10 inches in diameter, placing it on the greased baking sheet. Sprinkle the top of the loaf with sesame seeds; press the seeds gently into the surface of the loaf. Cover very loosely with plastic wrap; let the loaf rise until almost doubled in bulk, about 1 hour.

Place a rack in the center of the oven and preheat the oven to 425°F. Remove the plastic wrap. Bake the loaf in the center of the rack for 10 minutes. Lower the heat to 375°F and bake for 25 minutes. When the loaf is done, it will sound hollow when it's tapped on the bottom. Cool the loaf completely on a rack before slicing.

Cracklin' Herb Rolls

Dinner rolls are part of every Southerner's heritage, and on this subject New Orleanians are Southern as well as European, ever presenting our true origins according to what we truly want to eat. The herbs give these rolls a little lagniappe (that Creole "something extra"). Cracklin' (strips of fried pork fat or skin) weaves in a delicious country flavor.

Makes about 16 rolls

1 package active dry yeast (about 1 tablespoon)

1/4 cup lukewarm water (110°F)

1 cup milk

1/4 cup sugar

1/2 teaspoon salt

1/2 teaspoon garlic powder

1/2 cup vegetable shortening

3 1/4 cups all-purpose flour

1/4 teaspoon dried thyme

1/4 teaspoon dried rosemary

1/4 teaspoon dried oregano

2 eggs, beaten

1/2 cup pork cracklin', crumbled

In a small bowl, dissolve the yeast in the water. Scald the milk in a large saucepan over medium heat, then add the sugar, salt, garlic powder, and shortening. Add the flour and the dried herbs, mixing well. Add the eggs and yeast mixture. Beat until smooth, then incorporate the cracklin'. Cover the dough and let rise for about 1 hour. Coat the bottoms of small muffin tins with butter, fill each about half full with dough, and let rise until nearly doubled in size. Preheat the oven to 425°F. Bake the rolls until golden brown, about 25 minutes.

Black Pepper–Buttermilk Biscuits

Biscuits just aren't for breakfast, you know. In the South, they are offered at lunch or dinner, and you'd be wise to accept from time to time. And don't go thinking biscuits are boring until you've sampled these, with their kick of black pepper in the aftertaste.

....

Makes 16 biscuits

5 cups all-purpose flour

3 tablespoons sugar

1 tablespoon baking powder

1 teaspoon coarsely ground black pepper

1 teaspoon salt

1 teaspoon baking soda

3/4 cup vegetable shortening

1 package active dry yeast (about 1 tablespoon)

1/2 cup warm water (110°F)

2 cups buttermilk

Preheat the oven to 425°F. In a large bowl, mix together the flour, sugar, baking powder, pepper, salt, baking soda, and shortening until the mixture is the consistency of dry cornmeal. Dissolve the yeast in the warm water. When the yeast is white and bubbly, combine it with the buttermilk. Form a hole in the center of the dough and pour in the buttermilk, about one-fourth at a time, mixing well. Work the dough a little on a floured surface. Pat into a large circle about 3/8 inch thick. Cut out biscuits with a cutter and place on a nonstick baking sheet. Bake until golden brown on the outside and cooked on the inside, 10 to 12 minutes.

Hush Puppies

The Deep South story holds that these little balls of fried cornmeal batter got their name because they were tossed out the back kitchen door to silence the family dogs. "Hush, puppy!" Get it? The thing is, they work on the family every bit as well as they work on the family dogs. Hush puppies are traditionally served with any and all fried seafood, but they're great with any dish that makes you wish for a side of cornbread. For a real treat, put a few hush puppies in a bowl and ladle on your favorite étouffée.

Serves 8

3 cups cornmeal

1 cup all-purpose flour

2 teaspoons baking powder

1 teaspoon Creole seasoning (page 34)

4 eggs, beaten

2 medium onions, finely chopped

2 green onions, both white and green parts, finely chopped

About 1 cup milk

Vegetable oil for deep-frying

In a large bowl, mix the cornmeal, flour, baking powder, and Creole seasoning. Add the eggs, onions, and green onions. Slowly add the milk until the mixture slides gently off the mixing spoon.

Heat vegetable oil in a deep-fat fryer to 375°F. Drop teaspoons of the batter into the hot oil and fry until golden brown

Cornbread

Though sometimes we deny it, preferring the subtleties of our French-Spanish-African persona, New Orleans is also part of the Deep South. Therefore we love our cornbread, whenever we're not indulging in our French bread or crusty muffaletta loaf. Here's a basic recipe for cornbread that's sure to make you say "Yaw'l" just like we do.

Serves 6 to 8

2 eggs, slightly beaten

1 cup milk

1/4 cup unsalted butter, at room
    temperature

1 1/2 cups self-rising yellow cornmeal

1 cup self-rising flour

1/4 cup sugar

Preheat the oven to 450°F. Grease an 8- or 9-inch square baking pan. In a mixing bowl, combine the eggs, milk, butter, cornmeal, flour, and sugar. When thoroughly combined, pour the batter into the pan and bake until a toothpick inserted the center comes out clean, 20 to 25 minutes. Cut into squares and serve.

Cajun Confetti Cornbread

It wasn't too long ago that somebody in New Orleans had the notion of spicing up cornbread, and adding an extra dash of color while they were at it. The confetti confirms that there really is a party going on.

Serves 6 to 8

2 eggs, slightly beaten

1/4 cup unsalted butter, at room temperature

1 cup milk

1 1/2 cups self-rising yellow cornmeal

1 cup self-rising flour

1 jalapeño pepper, finely chopped

3 tablespoons finely chopped red bell pepper

3 tablespoons finely chopped green onion, both white and green parts

Preheat the oven to 350°F. Grease an 8- or 9-inch baking pan. Combine the eggs and butter in a mixing bowl, then add the milk. Stir in the cornmeal, flour, jalapeño and bell peppers, and green onion. Pour the batter into the prepared pan and bake until a toothpick inserted in the center comes out clean, 20 to 25 minutes. Cut into squares and serve.

Double Corn Muffins

This corn-y variation adds a little lagniappe to a standard corn muffin.

Serves 12

1¼ cups self-rising yellow cornmeal

1¼ cups self-rising flour

1 cup whole corn kernels

3 tablespoons finely chopped green
 onion, both white and green parts

¼ cup sugar

¼ cup unsalted butter, at room
 temperature

2 eggs, slightly beaten

1 cup milk

Preheat the oven to 450°F. Grease a 12-cup muffin tin. Combine the cornmeal, flour, corn, green onion, and sugar in a mixing bowl. Combine the butter, eggs, and milk in a separate bowl, then mix them thoroughly with the dry ingredients. Pour the batter evenly into the muffin tin and bake, until a toothpick inserted in the center of a muffin comes out clean, about 20 minutes.

Yam-Pecan Bread

Two terrific Louisiana loves, pecans and the sweet potatoes we call yams, join forces in this sweetish loaf bread. You can enjoy it for breakfast, as a snack, along with a savory meal, or even as a simple dessert.

Serves 8

3/4 cup unsalted butter, at room temperature

1 1/2 cups sugar

1/3 cup vegetable oil

5 eggs, lightly beaten

3 cups sifted all-purpose flour

3/4 teaspoon salt

2 1/2 teaspoons baking soda

3/4 cup chopped pecans

2 cups mashed canned Louisiana yams (sweet potatoes), 3/4 cup juice reserved for glaze

GLAZE

1/2 cup unsalted butter

1 cup sugar

3/4 cup juice from yams

Preheat the oven to 350°F. In a mixing bowl, using an electric mixer, cream together the butter, sugar, and vegetable oil, then add the eggs. In a separate bowl, mix the flour with the salt, baking soda, and pecans, then combine this with the creamed mixture. Add the mashed yams, incorporating thoroughly. Line the bottom of a tube pan with waxed paper and lightly grease the sides. Pour in the batter and bake until a knife inserted in the center comes out clean, 60 to 75 minutes.

About 15 minutes before the bread is done, melt the butter for the glaze in a small saucepan and stir in the sugar and yam juice. Boil until syrupy, about 5 minutes. Pour the glaze over the top of the bread as soon as it comes out of the oven. Let cool, then turn out onto a serving plate.

Spoonbread

Here's a traditional side dish, usually baked as a casserole, that wasn't lost upon the old Creoles of New Orleans. It's usually served in a bowl—and, yes, eaten with a spoon.

....

Serves 12

2 cups milk

2 cups water

2 cups cornmeal

2 teaspoons salt

4 egg yolks, beaten

4 egg whites, beaten until stiff

2 tablespoons baking powder

2 tablespoons unsalted butter

Preheat the oven to 425°F. Grease a 2-quart casserole dish. Combine the milk and water in a saucepan over medium heat. Add the cornmeal and salt, cooking for about 5 minutes. Add the egg yolks and whites, baking powder, and butter, stirring until the butter melts. Pour into the casserole dish and bake until a soft, moist bread is formed, about 40 minutes. Serve as a side dish.

Desserts

NEW ORLEANS BOWL COOKING FEATURES so many great dishes you might think we never save room for dessert. Well, we don't save, but we do tend to have. Honestly: when was the last time you ate so much you weren't the least bit tempted by the pie you pulled from the oven and set up on the windowsill to cool, or by the tray of diverse delectables some restaurant waiter held right under your nose? Good sense may or may not triumph, but you've got to admit—you want it!

Desserts in New Orleans range from plain to fancy, based on the great spectrum running from simple, everyday home meals to feasts in some of the most feast-friendly restaurants in the world. Gluttony doesn't really seem one of the seven deadly sins in New Orleans. It's usually treated more like one of the seven wonders of the world.

There are great puddings in New Orleans—led off by bread pudding, invented by some wonderful human being to use up day-old French bread. When you bake as much French bread as we do in New Orleans, whole armies could come and go and still leave some to be day-old. Once these loaves are turned into bread pudding, you understand that they may have found the happiest home of them all.

Did I mention that we really love ice cream? We do. We love it because it's cold and New Orleans is usually hot. We love it because it's rich and creamy, the way we like so many things in the course of a meal. And we love it because it sits so pretty beside a nice big wedge of pie or beneath a just-flambéed blanket of bananas Foster or some other classic New Orleans finale. Apparently, with the right amount of cream and the right amount of alcohol, even fire and ice can feel like your very best friends.

Bread Pudding

Mountains of leftover, sometimes even stale French bread must have threatened New Orleans' very survival from time to time. Why else would the city's cooks have worked so hard to take a boring dish and turn it into a local classic?

···

Serves 8 to 10

1 loaf stale French bread, broken up

1 cup sugar

$1/2$ teaspoon salt

1 (8-ounce) can fruit cocktail, with juice

$1/2$ teaspoon vanilla extract

1 cup raisins

2 tablespoons unsalted butter, melted

4 cups milk

WHISKEY SAUCE

1 tablespoon bourbon

$1/2$ cup unsalted butter

$1^1/2$ cups sugar

$1^1/2$ cups heavy cream

$3/4$ teaspoon ground nutmeg

$1/4$ teaspoon vanilla extract

Preheat the oven to 350°F. Grease a large 8 by 12-inch baking dish. Combine the bread, sugar, salt, fruit cocktail, vanilla, raisins, butter, and milk in a large bowl. Pour the mixture into the baking dish and bake until set, 35 to 40 minutes.

Make the sauce just before serving. In a medium saucepan, mix together the bourbon, butter, sugar, cream, nutmeg, and vanilla. Cook over medium-high heat until reduced by about half, about 5 minutes. Spoon about $1/4$ cup of sauce over each serving of bread pudding. Serve immediately.

Bananas Foster

This flaming dessert from Brennan's, named after the owner of a New Orleans awning company, is one of the city's sweetest signatures. Naturally, you can make bananas Foster without setting it on fire—if you're fearful of incinerating your kitchen or your guests. But if you're careful, it can be done without loss of life or limb. Just about every waiter in New Orleans lights bananas Foster all night long. And we're still around to share the recipe.

....

Serves 6

1 stick unsalted butter

1 (1-pound) box brown sugar

1 teaspoon ground cinnamon

4 ripe bananas, peeled and cut in half lengthwise

2 ounces white rum

Vanilla ice cream (optional)

In a large skillet, melt the butter. Stir in the brown sugar and cinnamon. Cook until the sugar begins to caramelize, about 5 minutes. Add the sliced bananas, turning to coat. Add the rum and set on fire over a gas flame or using a long match. Let the alcohol burn off. Place a banana on each plate. Spoon the sauce over the bananas. Serve warm. To serve à la mode, place a scoop of ice cream on each banana before spooning the sauce over.

Flaming Pontchatoula Strawberries

On the north shore of Lake Pontchartrain, the town of Pontchatoula is a sleepy, antique hunter's haven for most of any year. But during strawberry season, the place gets tired of waiting for guests and reaches deep into kitchens all over New Orleans. To make this dish, rely on your own local strawberries—the freshest, juiciest, and sweetest you can get your hands on.

Serves 4

1 pint fresh strawberries, trimmed
    and cut into 2 or 3 pieces each

¼ cup water

¼ cup sugar

¼ cup Grand Marnier

Vanilla ice cream

In a large sauté pan, combine the strawberries with the water and sugar over medium-high heat. Stir until the sauce thickens into a bright red syrup, then carefully add the Grand Marnier and set on fire over a gas flame or using a long match. Let the alcohol burn off, and spoon quickly into dessert bowls over vanilla ice cream

New Orleans Fig Cobbler

There was a time when just about every yard in New Orleans featured at least one fig tree. And if you didn't have one, your neighbor or aunt or brother-in-law did. When the figs came in, they really came in, and it was all you could do to invent ways of using them. Makers of preserves and jellies thrived more than most at such times, but surely cobblers like this one helped control the fig population explosion as well.

Serves 6

1/2 cup unsalted butter

1 cup all-purpose flour

1 cup sugar

1 cup milk

1 teaspoon baking soda

1 teaspoon salt

1/2 teaspoon ground nutmeg

1/2 teaspoon ground cinnamon

1 1/2 cups peeled fresh Mission or other
   purple-black figs

Preheat the oven to 350°F. Melt the butter in the bottom of a 1-quart baking dish, then mix in the flour, sugar, milk, baking soda, salt, nutmeg, and cinnamon to form a light batter. Arrange the figs on top of the batter and bake for 1 hour, until the top turns golden brown. Serve in a bowl.

Sweet Potato Pone

Louisiana yams are wonderful in this African-influenced pone. Think of it as a sweet potato pie, minus the crust.

....

Serves 10

5 large Louisiana yams (sweet potatoes)

1 cup unsalted butter, at room temperature

1 cup firmly packed brown sugar

5 eggs, beaten

1 cup milk

1/2 teaspoon ground cinnamon

1/4 teaspoon ground nutmeg

1/4 teaspoon salt

1/2 cup molasses

Zest of 1/2 orange

Zest of 1 lemon

Whipped cream

Preheat the oven to 350°F. Grease an 8 by 8-inch pan. Peel and grate the yams. In a large mixing bowl, using an electric mixer, cream together the butter and brown sugar. Blend in the eggs. Add the grated yams, milk, cinnamon, nutmeg, and salt, followed by the molasses and the orange and lemon zest. Pour into the pan and bake until set, about 1 hour. Spoon into bowls, and serve topped with whipped cream.

Rice Custard

Louisiana grows enough rice to sell the surplus to Asia, another part of the world that loves to eat our favorite starch. Since cooks in New Orleans often ended up with cooked rice left over in the days before the renewal powers of the microwave, they came up with plenty of rice desserts—like this simple, pleasing custard.

Serves 8 to 10

3/4 cup unsalted butter, at room temperature

1½ cups sugar

6 egg yolks, beaten

2¼ cups evaporated milk

2 tablespoons vanilla extract

3 cups cooked white rice

1/4 cup raisins

6 egg whites

1 or 2 teaspoons ground cinnamon

Preheat the oven to 300°F. Butter a 2½-quart baking dish. In a large mixing bowl, using an electric mixer, cream together the butter and sugar, then blend in the egg yolks, evaporated milk, and vanilla. Stir in the rice and the raisins. In a separate large bowl, beat the egg whites until stiff, then fold them into the rice mixture. Pour the custard into the baking dish and set this in a larger pan with water reaching about halfway up the side. Bake until a knife inserted in the center of the custard comes out clean, about 1 hour and 15 minutes. Serve in bowls, sprinkled with ground cinnamon.

Ruston Peach Rice Pudding

We know from visits to Atlanta, where every other street has the word "peach" in its name, that Georgia grows a few peaches from time to time—as do Deep South siblings Texas and Alabama. But any New Orleans cook worth his (or her) peach fuzz will pick the bright, explosively juicy orbs from the town of Ruston in north Louisiana any day of the week. If you've got some leftover cooked rice, here's the perfect dessert to spend it on.

Serves 8 to 10

1¹/₂ cups chopped Ruston peaches

¹/₂ cup golden raisins

1 cup firmly packed brown sugar

¹/₄ teaspoon salt

1¹/₂ teaspoons ground cinnamon

¹/₂ teaspoon ground ginger

¹/₈ teaspoon ground cloves

1 egg, beaten

1 teaspoon vanilla extract

1 (12-ounce) can evaporated milk

3 cups cooked rice

PEACH PECAN SAUCE

1 cup bottled or canned peach juice

¹/₄ cup firmly packed brown sugar

1 tablespoon cornstarch

¹/₂ cup chopped pecans

1 tablespoon unsalted butter

Preheat the oven to 350°F. Butter a 2¹/₂-quart baking dish. Combine the peaches, raisins, brown sugar, salt, spices, egg, and vanilla in a medium mixing bowl. Blend well, gradually adding the evaporated milk. Stir in the cooked rice and pour into the baking dish. Bake until the pudding is lightly browned and bubbly, 35 to 40 minutes.

Make the sauce just before serving. In a small saucepan, combine the peach juice, brown sugar, and cornstarch. Bring to a boil, stirring constantly, then lower the heat and simmer for 1 minute. Add the pecans and butter. Serve the pudding in bowls, topped with the sauce.

Pain Perdu

I love what the old Creoles called this dish: "lost bread." If it was ever lost (stale, over the hill, kaput), then it certainly was found by cooks who turned it into some of the best French toast the world has ever tasted.

Serves 2

4 eggs

1 teaspoon vanilla extract

1/4 cup milk

1/2 teaspoon ground allspice

1/4 cup unsalted butter

6 slices 1-inch-thick day-old French bread

Powdered sugar

In a large bowl, beat together the eggs, vanilla, milk, and allspice. Melt the butter in a large skillet over medium heat. Soak the bread slices in the egg mixture on both sides, soaking up all of the mixture. Fry in the butter on both sides until golden brown, about 10 minutes. Place 3 slices on each plate. Sprinkle generously with powdered sugar.

Pralines and Cream

The brown sugar and pecan confections called pralines used to be sold on the streets by Creole women carrying baskets of them and wearing colorful bandanas called tignons. Today, you can find pralines almost anywhere in New Orleans. And you can also make them pretty easily. Maybe best of all, you can make them halfway and then spoon them hot over ice cream. That's what's this dessert is all about.

Serves 10

2 cups firmly packed brown sugar
1 cup granulated sugar
1 cup heavy cream
1 cup water
1 teaspoon vanilla extract
3 cups chopped pecans
Vanilla ice cream

In a large saucepan, combine the sugars, cream, water, and vanilla. Cook until the mixture forms a soft ball when you drop a little in some cold water (238°F). Remove the pan from the heat and beat the mixture until it is creamy. Stir in the pecans. Spoon over bowls of vanilla ice cream.

Grand Isle Couche-Couche

Although this cornmeal pudding could serve as a dessert, most New Orleanians who like couche-couche prefer it for breakfast, splashed with a bit of cold milk. The Cajuns of Grand Isle learned to make it from the Indians when the great interaction called Louisiana first started bubbling in the pan.

Serves 6

2 cups cornmeal
1 teaspoon salt
1 egg
1 teaspoon baking soda
1 cup hot milk
1 teaspoon vegetable oil
Cold milk

Mix the cornmeal, salt, egg, and baking soda with the hot milk in a bowl. Lightly coat a large skillet or pan with the oil, and pour in the cornmeal mixture. Cook, stirring with a fork, over medium heat for about 30 minutes, until thickened. Serve in bowls with cold milk.

Index

New Orleans Seafood Cookbook

by Andrew Jaeger and John DeMers

It's impossible to think about New Orleans cuisine without thinking seafood—soft-shelled crab, catfish, swordfish, oysters, shrimp, speckled trout, snapper, blue crab, and even shark. And it's impossible for anyone in New Orleans to think about seafood without thinking of Andrew Jaeger, third-generation seafood chef and proprietor of the famous New Orleans restaurant. This book presents some 125 of his best-loved recipes, lavishly illustrated with full-color photos. It's all you need to have your own personal Mardi Gras.

7 3/8 x 9 1/4 inches, 224 pages
$19.95 paper with flaps (Can $31.95)
ISBN 1-58008-0624-2

Oysters

by John DeMers and Andrew Jaeger

What can a poor boy and a Rockefeller have in common? If you're thinking of that bodacious bivalve beloved in the Big Easy, you're absolutely right. John DeMers and Andrew Jaeger have joined forces for the best little book on this slippery subject. For the experienced oyster connoisseur or the enthusiastic novice who just wants to slurp 'em down raw, *Oysters* offer essentials for purchasing, cleaning, and shucking, along with plenty of serving suggestions. Try them sautéed, smoked, stewed, grilled, barbecued, baked, fried, or po' boyed.

5 x 6 inches, 96 pages
$4.95 paper (Can $7.95)
ISBN 0-89087-869-2

MORE NEW ORLEANS COOKBOOKS FROM TEN SPEED PRESS

The Heaven on Seven Cookbook
Where It's Mardi Gras All the Time!
by Jimmy Bannos and John DeMers

When Jimmy Bannos started experimenting with Louisiana cooking, he transformed his Chicago coffee shop into the best Cajun restaurant north of the Mason-Dixon line. Jimmy is still serving up bowl after bowl of steaming gumbo, not to mention the most original Creole creations imaginable.

"Jimmy Bannos' homage to the cooking of New Orleans is heartfelt and peppered with spicy delights. Some are adaptations of Crescent City classics and others are Heaven on Seven originals. Taken together, they provide an opportunity to enjoy heaven on earth."
—WILLIAM RICE, *Chicago Tribune*

7 3/8 x 9 1/8 inches, inches, 192 pages
$24.95 hardcover (Can $39.95)
ISBN 1-58008-168-1

Dominique's Fresh Flavors
Cooking with Latitude in New Orleans
by Dominique Macquet and John DeMers

What can you expect from a chef raised on Mauritius, who apprenticed in South Africa, traveled extensively within Latin and Asian cultures, mastered California cuisine as a Beverly Hills chef, and now runs his own restaurant in New Orleans? Take it from legendary chef Jean-Louis Palladin: "A fabulous tour of global cuisine!" In *Dominique's Fresh Flavors*, Dominique Macquet explores exotic culinary frontiers with the expertise and grounding of a classically trained French chef.

7 15/16 x 8 7/8 inches, 208 pages
$27.95 hardcover (Can $45.00)
ISBN 1-58008-153-3

Available at your local bookstore, or order directly from us at:

Ten Speed Press / Celestial Arts
P.O. Box 7123, Berkeley, CA 94707
Phone (800) 841-2665 / Fax (510) 559-1629
order@tenspeed.com / www.tenspeed.com